BURKE COUNTY
NORTH CAROLINA

BURKE COUNTY
NORTH CAROLINA

HISTORIC TALES FROM THE
GATEWAY TO THE BLUE RIDGE

LARRY R. CLARK

Charleston — London

History
PRESS

Published by The History Press
Charleston, SC 29403
www.historypress.net

First published 2007

Manufactured in the United Kingdom

ISBN 978.1.59629.323.6

Library of Congress Cataloging-in-Publication Data
Clark, Larry R., 1940-
  Burke County, North Carolina : historic tales from the Gateway to the Blue Ridge / Larry
R. Clark.
     p. cm.
  ISBN-13: 978-1-59629-323-6 (alk. paper) 1. Burke County (N.C.)--History--Anecdotes.
2. Burke County (N.C.)--Biography--Anecdotes. 3. Burke County (N.C.)--History, Local--
Anecdotes. I. Title.
  F262.B96C58 2007
  975.6'85--dc22
                              2007037723

Contents

CONTENTS

Introduction

For over a decade now I've regularly submitted columns (I call them "stories") to our local newspaper, the *News Herald*. Many of these have been personal tales about the joys of living in Burke County, and especially along the banks of Irish Creek at the foot of Table Rock Mountain. And, of course, I've written about grandchildren and our children and life in general—but I've also been fascinated with the many stories, legends and myths told about Burke County's past. The following pages contain a selected collection of these published *News Herald* articles that, hopefully, will provide you with vivid images of Burke and its people.

Situated at the headwaters of the majestic Catawba River, Burke County has been greatly influenced by geography. Throughout much of its history, this region served as a passageway to and from the nearby Blue Ridge Mountains and existed as a wild and rough frontier well into the nineteenth century. Following the Native American, Spanish and earliest settlers who came to this land, Burke County was created on June 1, 1777, from a divided Rowan County. Thereafter, all or part of seventeen western North Carolina counties were carved from "Old" Burke's original boundaries.

Native Americans occupied this region for thousands of years before the first Europeans arrived, most likely the soldiers of Spaniard Hernando de Soto around 1540. Archaeologists have only recently begun to piece together the lost story of a native Catawba American Indian village and Fort San Juan constructed along Warrior Fork in 1567 by soldiers of Captain Juan Pardo—some twenty years before Sir Walter Raleigh's "Lost Colony" on Roanoke Island and forty years earlier than the founding of Jamestown in Virginia. This is the exciting "stuff" of a people's heritage that makes local history so important to record and share with future generations.

For the most part, Burke County was settled by English, Welsh, Scottish, Irish and German immigrants during the early eighteenth century. It is their fortitude in carving communities out of virgin forest and their determination and heroic efforts during the American War for Independence from the British Crown that explains, in part, the people of Burke today. And then there are stories about the 1830s gold rush, the War Between the States and, thereafter, the rise of a timber industry, textiles and furniture manufacturing. The arrival of America's last colonists, the Waldensians from northern Italy, added another important and special character to Burke's heritage as the twentieth century brought new challenges and dramatic changes.

Burke County, North Carolina: Historic Tales from the Gateway to the Blue Ridge should only be your introduction to the people, places and events that influenced this region of western North Carolina. For a more complete account of Burke County history and families, you must examine the premier work of Edward W. Phifer Jr. in *The History of a North Carolina County: Burke* and the two volumes of *The Heritage of Burke County* published by the Burke County Historical Society. Other important sources of information may be observed or found at the restored Old County Courthouse and the McDowell House maintained by the Historic Burke Foundation. You may also want to visit the Waldensian Heritage Museum and Trail of Faith, the Burke County Library's North Carolina Room along with the History Museum of Burke County and its railway exhibits at Morganton's recently renovated Greene Street Railroad Depot.

From this, I hope you learn to appreciate the people and county of Burke as I do.

Indian, Spanish, English, Irish, Scottish, Welsh, African, German

Native Americans occupied this rugged mountain land at least ten thousand years before the first Europeans arrived. Sometime around two thousand years ago, these "Indians" began building towns along streams and rivers to farm the rich bottomlands. By the time Christopher Columbus arrived in the West Indies, western North Carolina was populated primarily by two aboriginal groups, the Siouan speaking Catawba along the river valleys and the Iroquoian related Cherokee in the high mountains. Various estimates place their numbers ca.1500 at around forty thousand. The Cherokee and Catawba American Indians ultimately became the local native tribes of history and became the people who taught Europeans how to survive in this woodland wilderness. In turn, it was the Europeans who brought the diseases of smallpox and measles that killed perhaps half the Native American population in western North Carolina by 1700, a pandemic that almost wiped out the Catawba.

Burke's European heritage began in the sixteenth century with the appearance of Spanish conquistadors and a fort along Warrior Fork. In fact, the arrival of Captain Juan Pardo and his soldiers in 1566 and the construction of Fort San Juan predate the coming of English settlers by almost two centuries. Therefore it is the Spanish who were the first to arrive in North Carolina. Before Pardo, it is likely that Hernando de Soto's expedition passed through the Catawba Valley region some twenty-five years earlier on his way to the Mississippi River.

With the arrival of English colonists along the mid-Atlantic coast during the seventeenth century, there is little doubt that many an adventuresome hunter and trader passed along the Catawba River seeking profitable trade for American Indian furs and hides. Later, western North Carolina became

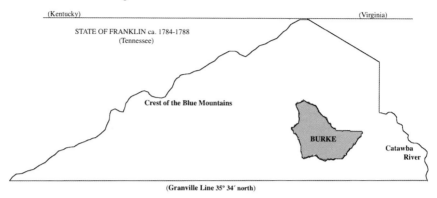

Original Old Burke Boundries June 1, 1777

Created on June 1, 1777, a much larger Burke County followed rivers and mountains to intersect with the Granville Line at latitude 35° 34′ north. By 1834 all or part of seventeen western North Carolina counties were taken from its original boundary. This map also depicts the "State of Franklin," an illegal state created by local residents in 1785 with John Sevier as "governor." *Author Collection*

part of the Earl of Granville's district, which meant that royal agents and surveyors in the east had to certify all land grants in these parts. As a young man, John Perkins (who lived in present-day Catawba County) received a land grant along "John's River" as payment for his services as guide and hunter to prospective buyers.

One such customer was the German bishop, Spangenberg, who traveled the Catawba River in search of land suitable for a Moravian colony. Spangenberg, however, chose not to claim this wilderness land with its wolves and returned east to found Salem near present-day Winston-Salem. Spangenberg's 1752 journal, however, provides us with the first written descriptions of what would soon become Old Burke. Thereafter, the French and Indian War of 1753–1763 discouraged other pioneers to settle, and many families in the region retreated elsewhere to escape Native American raiders.

Burke County was created at the beginning of the American Revolution on June 1, 1777, from Rowan County as a large region that encompassed all of northwest North Carolina, and some will say, portions of eastern Tennessee. In fact Old Burke eventually became the "Mother County" to all or part of seventeen North Carolina counties. In *The History of a County: Burke*, Edward Phifer reports that 1,856 land claims were recorded from 1778–1780, although many were speculators who never intended to live here. The population of this new, large county is estimated at less than four thousand people during the years of revolution, 1775–1783. With English guns and powder, their Cherokee allies raided American Patriot farms from Virginia to Georgia. Joint military campaigns by Virginia, North Carolina and Georgia destroyed many Cherokee villages in the Appalachian Mountains and soon ended this threat to the region.

Into the next century, Old Burke's population fluctuated greatly as other counties were carved from its lands. These divisions explain, in part, why Burke County had fewer than ten thousand people (white and black) recorded in the 1860 U.S. census. Elder Springs (later Morganton), as the only community of any size, assumed the duty of county seat and served as the state's six-county judicial district of Morgan. During the twice yearly North Carolina Superior Court meetings, people arrived from far and wide to live in tent camps and attend these very public trials. As one circuit judge remarked about these festive frontier gatherings, "I do not know any rival for this place in regard to drunkenness, ignorance, superstition and the most brutal debauchery."[1]

The first Africans to arrive in Old Burke were the slaves of pioneer families such as the Averys, McDowells, Erwins and Greenlees, although this county never obtained a "Gone with the Wind" plantation status like the eastern lowlands. It should also be noted that these slaves were not likely newly arrived Africans just off the boats, as they had been introduced into American colonies by the British Crown more than a hundred years earlier. As elsewhere in the Old South, North Carolina politicians wrote restrictive slave laws, ministers quoted the Bible in support of slavery, slave owners espoused the advantages of this "peculiar institution" and the average white citizen knew no other custom.

The first U.S. census of 1790 recorded slightly more than 1,200 heads of households in Old Burke, a statistic which translates into a total county population, including slaves, free Negroes, females and children, somewhere around 8,000 people. Phifer estimates that slaves comprised 7 percent of this total in 1790 and never more than 26 percent in later years. Prior to the War for Southern Independence, the average Burke slaveholder had fewer than ten slaves and only a few dozen families ever possessed fifty or more. Several local African Americans actually gained their freedom, since the 1860 census listed 225 free Negroes in Burke out of some 2,300 total. Burke's typical slave, therefore, was not a "farmhand," since many could be found at skilled work in mining, cottage manufactures, private households, public works and the growing timber industry. In most respects both whites and blacks in Burke County were "dirt-poor farmers" during the colonial and early modern eras.

Table Rock—A Gateway to the Blue Ridge Mountains

Anyone traveling into or out of Burke County with their eyes open in the daytime has seen that flat-topped mountain, which we call Table Rock. It's hard to miss this ancient "rock" from many vantage points. Fred Acuff, a geology instructor at the local community college, described the formation of this mountain in Phifer's book as some four hundred million years old from the Paleozoic Era—the same period in which nearby Mt. Mitchell, Grandfather Mountain and the Appalachian chain were born. During these spectacular upheavals, Table Rock was created along with Shortoff (with its four-hundred-foot cliff), Hawksbill, the Chimneys and Long Arm at over 4,300 feet. Table Rock, in fact, could be the core of a prehistoric volcano. Added to this spectacular event, some two thousand feet below Table Rock's western face lies Linville Gorge and Linville River, an impressive twelve-mile-long cut through granite.

There's little doubt that both Native Americans and early European pioneers sighted this auspicious peak with its location near the headwaters of the Catawba River. Thousands of years ago American Indians settled along the rich bottomlands of the river and its tributaries. The Spanish wrote about the "Blue Mountains," and in 1752 Bishop Spangenberg visited near "Table Mountain." While no one seems to know when the name "Table Rock" first came into use, Linville River and the gorge, on the other hand, were named for William Linville who lived in the area during the eighteenth century. He and his son were killed there by hostile Native Americans.

We think our mountain is rather unique. An Internet search found Table Rock Lake near Branson, Missouri, and a Table Rock State Park in South Carolina near Greenville. But neither of these rocks come close to our spectacular Table Rock rising over three thousand feet into a Carolina blue

Rising over three thousand feet above the county, Table Rock Mountain has attracted attention from pioneers, botanists, artists and writers for centuries. Some two thousand feet below its western cliffs lay a river and Linville Gorge, a twelve-mile-long cut into ancient granite that today is a National Wilderness Area. *Author Collection.*

sky. I also found in my research that "The Table Rock" of Burke County is not to be found or listed on any search—not even in North Carolina tourism sites. It seems that our magnificent mountain has been absorbed into the Linville Gorge National Wilderness Area, where the first Internet listing for "Linville Gorge" only mentioned Table Rock and then described it as being in Montana! Even Outward Bound, that international organization with over 650 adventure expeditions worldwide (and housed on the side of Table Rock for decades) doesn't mention Table Rock—or even Linville Gorge for that matter. For their North Carolina adventures, Outward Bound describes "expeditions into the Appalachian wilderness." By the way, Linville Gorge (of Burke County) is the *only* wilderness area in North Carolina.

Someone should tell these folks that they have missed a golden opportunity to promote Table Rock as the most visible symbol of the region. Located in Pisgah National Forest, the U.S. Forest Service tends to "the Rock" as part of its mandate to preserve environmental treasures for all people. Created in 1964, the Linville Gorge Wilderness Area has now grown to almost twelve thousand acres and gained national fame as the "Grand Canyon of the East." Likewise, Table Rock has a national reputation for being the best place to rock climb anywhere in the southeastern United States; however, rock climbing on Table Rock officially ended in April 2006 due to environmental concerns. Those who seek such pleasures will now have to scale selected rocky cliffs in the gorge.

With a fairly nice gravel road to a parking lot near the top, Table Rock also attracts attention with its hiking trails and camping areas, picnic tables and beautiful scenery. As part of the Southern Appalachian Mountains, it's famous for the varied floras found by famous French botanist André Michaux in the eighteenth century and John Fraser, a Scottish botanist, in the nineteenth century. He's the one who collected *carex fraseri* (Fraser's sedge) on the banks of the Catawba River near "Table Mountain." There are also reports that several "extinct" animal species have returned to the mountain, for example: the eagle, falcon, coyote, turkey, an occasional bear and, perhaps, the mountain lion. Contrary to certain Internet sources and the Hollywood movie, this mountain also has an international reputation with Jules Verne's last novel, *The Master of the World*, in which he described the "Great Eyrie" (Table Rock, of course) rising high above the valley to sometimes belch strange sounds and fire over the little village of Morganton.

Burke Countians can go picnicking, hiking, camping and/or sightseeing for free anytime—although it's best to wander these trails in winter when the leaves are off the trees. Take the one-mile walk to the top of Table Rock from the parking area and see spectacular views on clear days. If you really get excited about walking, you can follow the nearby Mountains-to-the-Sea Trail and, you guessed it, see the Atlantic Ocean, or stop off at the bottom of Table Rock and visit the State Fish Hatchery. All you need do is give yourself a day to drive north on highway 181 about twenty miles from Morganton to Gingercake, turn left and left again following the Table Rock signs. There are a couple of other ways to get up the mountain—but you don't want to go there. Be careful. The gravel road has many sharp turns and two-way traffic.

Get out of the house! Enjoy Burke County's extra special landscape. In many ways, Table Rock and the surrounding mountains and waterways shaped and defined this county and its people. With all of this geography, there's little wonder why Table Rock became a common name and symbol among area businesses and government agencies—and that Burke County was once advertised as a "Gateway to the Blue Ridge."

Native Americans of
Western North Carolina[2]

At the end of the last Ice Age around fifteen thousand years ago, western North Carolina's climate consisted of cool summers, bitter winters and perhaps spots of permanent snow on its highest mountains. Archaeological studies along the headwaters of the Catawba River reveal the presence of Paleo-Indians in the region who most likely were migratory and visited only to hunt the bison, elk, bear, deer and occasional caribou. These first people of Burke also shared these game animals with the wolf, mountain lion and coyote.

At some point during the Archaic Period 8000–1000 BC, Native Americans adapted to a more moderate environment as a dominant evergreen forest was slowly replaced with deciduous trees and their abundant nuts and acorns. Local rivers and streams contained fish, turtles and mussels, while the sky above was heavy with pigeons, geese, ducks and doves. With abundant food supplies, Native American populations increased beyond the small, nomadic bands of earlier millennia and offered an opportunity for "permanent" seasonal camps where they returned year after year. These highly skilled forest and river people developed new technologies that significantly improved their lives. The atlatl, or throwing stick, increased accuracy with a short spear that proved advantageous in thick forest. The spokeshave, nutting stone, hand drill, awl, soapstone bowl and grooved ax are other common artifacts of this period. Archaic sites typically contain numerous stone flakes used as scrappers and blades.

A significant cultural revolution occurred for these people during the Woodland Period, 1000 BC–AD 1500 . The hoe and stone grinder signaled the arrival of gardening in the rich valley soils of the Catawba River Valley. Corn, pumpkin and squash were harvested and then stored for winter months in clay vessels. This renewable food supply encouraged the

Known as a "people of the river," the Catawba American Indians occupied rich bottomlands of the upper Catawba River basin centuries before European settlers arrived. Their gardens produced ample corn, beans, squash and pumpkin to support villages with populations into the hundreds. *Internet graphic. Catawba Corn Festival (1913). Rock Hill, South Carolina. 10 July 2000.*

establishment of long-term villages with substantial housing constructed of poles covered with grass thatch and woven walls packed in clay. The typical prehistoric pottery of Burke County is constructed of a fine clay material, brown to gray-black in color, mixed with crushed soapstone and most often decorated in a curvilinear stamped pattern. Apparently unique to the upper Catawba River Basin, researcher Robert Keeler classified this pottery as the Burke Series. Thousands of broken pottery fragments have been found, along with several small, complete pots with pointed bases that apparently required ground holes to set upright.

Woodland sites in Burke occasionally reveal soapstone and clay pipes, decorative stone or shell gorgets and polished stone ax heads (or celts). Invention of the bow and arrow during this cultural phase probably indicates a greater dependency on hunting small game. Spear points tend to be small, and the tiny "bird points" were used with a blowgun dart. During the later part of the Woodland Period, the development of agriculture spawned even larger villages throughout our region, some fortified with palisades constructed from logs. Certain villages appear to have served as ceremonial centers with special buildings built atop human-made earthen mounds. Chiefdoms, tribes, extensive trade, complex religious customs and warfare indicated a complex social, economic and political lifestyle.

The historic period began for Native Americans as each tribe came into contact with European explorers and colonists. By the time Christopher Columbus arrived in the West Indies, western North Carolina was primarily populated by two aboriginal linguistic groups, the Souian speaking Catawba along the river valleys and the Iroquoian related Cherokee in surrounding mountains and foothills. Various estimates place their total population at around forty thousand people. The first Europeans to travel in what was to become Burke County were the Spanish expeditions of Hernando de Soto in 1540, and over two decades later, Captain Juan Pardo in 1566. A Native American uprising in 1568 ended Spain's attempt to colonize the Carolina backcountry.

Europeans did not return to the region for more than a century as English trappers and traders came from their coastal colonies. Virginians established the Trading Path, or Occoneechee Trail, between Petersburg and the Catawba and Cherokee towns in the Carolinas to barter their knives, axes, hoes, cloth, guns and powder for American Indian furs, hides, food and slaves. An interesting anomaly appears in this story as English travellers into the Catawba Valley found no Native American villages. While there is a legend of a past war between the Cherokee and Catawba that resulted in this region being designated as a common hunting ground with no villages permitted, one historic fact is that the first Europeans introduced the deadly diseases of smallpox and measles among the American Indians. It has been estimated that fully one-half of the native population died from such plagues.

During the American Revolution, the Catawba chose to join the colonists while the Cherokee became mercenaries for the British army. Cherokee raiding parties attacked towns and farms across the western frontier. In May 1777, when the county of Burke was created, the state of North Carolina decreed a bounty of £15 for each Cherokee prisoner of war and £10 for each Native American scalp. Joint military campaigns conducted by North Carolina, Virginia and South Carolina against the Cherokee resulted in the destruction of some forty villages. The treaty signed that summer moved the "Indian Boundary" from the Catawba Valley and redrew it in the Blue Ridge Mountains—which removed all American Indian claims to this region.

Nature's Little Secrets Along the Catawba River

I finally did something that had been in my daydreams for years—and did it twice! The daydream was to canoe down the Catawba River and take photographs of native flora and fauna. But reality was a little different from the dream. First, I actually made these trips with the benefit of an old, small fishing boat and motor (7.5hp) on loan from my son-in-law, and second, I discovered that I have a lot to learn about taking photographs out in the wilderness. However, I'll take my daydreams any way I can get them.

The boat launch site on John's River off Highway 18 North is not the most appealing in Burke County (now much improved), but it is convenient. Trucks and automobiles roar overhead as they cross the John's River Bridge and their fumes drift down over the water. All of these unnatural things quickly fade behind as you putt-putt downstream to see what you will see. With no wind the dark water is as smooth and shiny as obsidian glass. When the John's level is high, giant trees of sycamore, tulip poplar, river birch and maple drape their towering limbs across the sky and gently dip leaves into the water. If you turn off the boat's motor and drift, a most gratifying thing happens. You hear the pure, unfiltered silence of Mother Nature wrapping you in her cloak of quiet solitude.

Entering the Catawba River is a different experience. The river stretches wide, maybe two hundred yards across at this juncture, with a bright Carolina blue sky overhead. Only a drifting leaf or limb lets you know that these shallow waters are leisurely flowing out of the mountains to the west then eastward and south across South Carolina as the Santee and Wateree rivers to eventually enter the Atlantic Ocean. During my second trip on the Catawba its waters were a reddish brown (not a pretty sight) from upstream runoff due to recent heavy rains. In fact, the boat's propeller seemed to be churning chocolate pudding. I'm certain the fish and birds do not enjoy these days.

As construction began on the Lake James dams, the Great Flood of 1916 hit. Local streams and the Catawba River overflowed their banks and caused considerable damage. No lives were lost, but several houses and businesses were flooded, such as Allman's Blacksmith Shop. *Burke County Public Library, Picture Burke Collection. Wayne Hitt.*

The impoundment of Lake James required construction of three dams between 1916 and 1923. Other than manpower, thousands of tons of earth and rock were moved by horses and mules along with an occasional steam locomotive and a steam powered excavator. *Committee for the Preservation of Black History in Burke County.*

If you turn right into the Catawba you travel upriver toward Quaker Meadows and Highway 181. This is not a good idea for me, since large sandbars snag even small, shallow draft boats. Turn left and you can travel several miles into Lake Rhodhiss, stopping at Rhodhiss Dam to imagine the mighty Catawba River descending into Catawba County's Lake Hickory and beyond. Although my photographs were generally quite poor, "Kodak moments" abound at many locations. I was surprised at the number of turtles, a half dozen at a time, basking on logs and rocks along the riverbanks, sunlight gleaming on their smooth shells. These nervous critters will not let you within one hundred feet before sliding into the water. Birds seem to be even less inclined to pose for the camera. Several times I drifted silently toward a great blue heron only to capture a blur and become grounded near the bank. This majestic blue-gray wader stands about four feet tall with a wingspan of four feet (the same as an eagle). In flight, its long neck is folded back into an "S" with slender legs trailing behind—a beautiful bird that appears to fly in slow motion.

Another large bird seen on the river, brilliant white in color, was likely an American egret. One really neat discovery was the kingfisher flittering from one side of the river to the other, chattering a loud, high-pitched call. Somewhat larger than a blue jay, with a slight resemblance, the blue-gray and white kingfisher plunges into the water for a quick meal. Its large head sports a ragged crest of fluffy feathers that provides a modern hippie look. At a distance, several species of woodpeckers and ducks were also seen or heard. The most interesting wildlife spotted, I thought, was the cormorant, which I first thought was a loon. The cormorant, however, is totally black with a wingspan of almost three feet and a long snake-like neck. I came upon a flock of these birds, perched on the limbs of a submerged tree, and watched as their wings beat the water before becoming airborne.

Before the chill of winter sets in I do hope to get the little boat (and my camera) back to John's River and the Catawba, and perhaps onto Lake James. It's really marvelous to know that such splendid patches of solitude are to be found in our own backyard. Part of my new daydream now includes taking a few grandchildren along. Now that could be a real adventure. The thought also comes to mind that perhaps we should do this sooner rather than later given the current popularity with housing developments along Burke County's waterfront property.

Which reminds me that we should never forget that each generation must seek to preserve our natural resources for future generations. If not us, then who will? To quote the great American poet Ralph Waldo Emerson, "This time, like all times, is a very good one, if we but know what to do with it."

Way Back When Burke Was Part of Spanish Florida

*B*uenos diás, mis amigos y amigas! Strange to think about, but the land we now call Burke County was once upon a time part of Florida—or La Florida to be correct. This story begins when Spain discovered a "new world" back in 1492. Christopher Columbus, an Italian sailing for the king and queen of Spain, arrived in the Caribbean islands believing he had found a western ocean route to the spices of India. The natives Columbus found, therefore, became known as "Indians," and these Caribbean islands were, thereafter, marked on maps as the "West Indies." Spain sent more ships and conquistadors to explore and claim this land for their rapidly growing empire, soon to become the largest in the history of the world. During the first half of the sixteenth century Spanish soldiers, merchants, priests and colonists pushed the American Indians aside to conquer and settle *Nuevo España* that stretched from Mexico to the tip of South America.

The first European towns to be built in the Americas included Havana, Cuba (1515), Mexico City (1521), Lima, Peru (1535) and Santiago, Chile (1541). The peninsula of La Florida was discovered in 1513 by Juan Ponce de León, then governor of Puerto Rico. Later, the Spanish village of St. Augustine was founded on the Atlantic coast, the first permanent European settlement in North America and today its oldest city. In 1540 Hernando de Soto traveled from the Gulf of Mexico across the southeastern United States (including western North Carolina) and then westward to discover the Mississippi River. After this, Spain's attention turned to the exploration and colonization of a vast region from Florida to Chesapeake Bay and west to the "Blue Mountains" of the Appalachians. This area of the southeastern United States was known to Spain as *La Florida*. Spain financed these expeditions with an abundance of gold, silver and gems shipped home from Mexico and South America for the glory of empire, God and king.

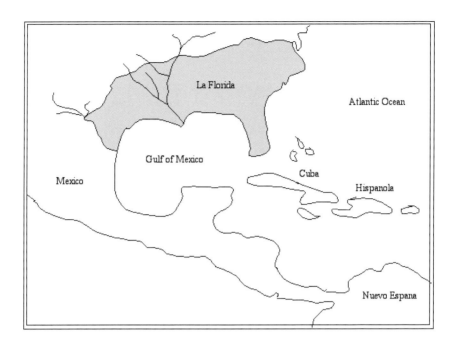

In 1566 Spanish Captain Juan Pardo led an expedition into western North Carolina to claim land for King Phillip II. Known as *La Florida*, this region of the southeastern United States was for a brief time part of the Spanish Empire. Spain's attempts failed and a century passed before English colonists arrived. *Author Collection.*

Captain General Pedro Menéndez de Avilés was responsible to King Philip II of Spain for exploring the southeast Atlantic coast, removing French Huguenot colonies, founding the first permanent North American town, St. Augustine, and sending expeditions into western North Carolina. *Author's photograph of color ceramic tile portrait at the City of St. Augustine Museum, Florida.*

In order to achieve these ambitious goals, King Philip II appointed Pedro Menéndez de Avilés as *adelantado* and captain general of La Florida. Menéndez was well known in this Catholic empire as the man who destroyed Protestant French Huguenot colonies along the south Atlantic coast. During one such battle following the Spanish capture of Fort Caroline (near Jacksonville), Menéndez hanged all its defenders in nearby trees "not as Frenchmen but as heretics."[3]

Captain General Menéndez designated Santa Elena, South Carolina, (currently on Parris Island) as the capital of La Florida. His three-year contract with King Philip required the establishment of at least four towns on the Atlantic coast and the importation of five hundred settlers. His efforts to expand northward along the Carolina coast to Chesapeake Bay were constantly stymied by "the desert islands" and storms off these outer banks. Therefore, Menéndez developed a plan to move inland, build forts and construct a road from Santa Elena to the silver mines of Mexico.

The man selected to follow the trail of Soto into the Blue Mountains of western North Carolina was Captain Juan Pardo, a career soldier summoned from St. Augustine along with 250 soldiers. Menéndez's orders were simple: pacify and Christianize the Native Americans (by force if necessary) and accept their lands in the name of His Royal Catholic Majesty King Phillip II and the pope, as God's high priest on earth.

The American Indians, now considered to be loyal subjects of Spain, were instructed to provide food as tribute and "volunteer" labor to all officials and soldiers of His Majesty. In addition, Catholic priests came into their villages to instruct them in Holy Scripture and the Christian faith. This system worked very well for decades among Central and South American Indians but the Spanish soon realized that the Native Americans of the Blue Mountains were different. In December 1566 Captain Pardo and 125 of his soldiers began their first journey north along the Wateree, Santee and "Cuttawa" rivers to find the native village of Joara and claim the lands along the headwaters of the Catawba River (Burke County) for Spain.

And we've only learned of this amazing bit of history in the past few years as archaeologists continue to excavate Joara and a Spanish fort on the Berry's farm along Warrior Fork. But, hey, that's another story to be told later.

Captain Juan Pardo and the Spanish Empire

Way back when the Spanish Empire reached into the mountains of western North Carolina, Captain General Pedro Menéndez de Avilés at the capital of La Florida in Santa Elena (Parris Island, South Carolina), dreamed of colonizing the southern United States from Chesapeake Bay to the Blue Ridge Mountains and ultimately into Mexico. In 1566 Menéndez ordered Captain Juan Pardo to march north with 125 soldiers to pacify the natives and claim this land for King Philip II. Along the way, Pardo visited a number of Native American towns where he met many chiefs and delivered an official speech that declared:

> We require you to understand these rules: that you acknowledge the Catholic Church superior of the whole world, and its high priest called the Pope, and in his name the King of Spain as lords of this land by virtue of your donation.[4]

Within seventeen days Pardo and his troops arrived in the native town of Joara (Burke County) in December along the headwaters of the Catawba River. With his westward passage blocked by deep snows on the Blue Ridge Mountains, Pardo ordered the construction of Fort San Juan and made plans to explore other native villages in the region. Fort San Juan, therefore, became the first European structure and occupation to be recorded in North Carolina history—more than twenty years earlier than the "lost" English colony on Roanoke Island and forty years before the James Towne settlement in Virginia.

Archaeological excavations in Burke over the past several years have determined that Joara was a large late-Mississippian town that could have supported several hundred people with fields of maize (corn), hunting,

Since the 1980s archaeologist Dr. David Moore has conducted excavations at the Berry farm on a sixteenth-century Catawba American Indian village. In recent years, this site also revealed the floors of burned cabins and Spanish artifacts. These remains are believed to be Fort San Juan constructed by the soldiers of Captain Juan Pardo in 1567. *Author Collection.*

fishing and food collecting. Most likely these "people of the river" were kin to the historic Catawba American Indians and Joara was the village of "Xuala" visited by Hernando de Soto some twenty-five years earlier.

Sergeant Hernando Moyano de Morales and thirty men were left behind at Fort San Juan while Pardo traveled east along the Catawba River to the villages of Quinahaqui and Guatari. Pardo remained at this last town for over two weeks and in late February received a message from Santa Elena to return immediately and prepare for a possible invasion by the French. Father Sebastian and four soldiers remained in Guatari to oversee the construction of another fort, along with corncribs and a guesthouse for future Spanish visits. Burdened with corn tribute from local villages, Pardo traveled south to arrive in Santa Elena by early April. The threatened attack by France never came.

Meanwhile, back in Burke, Sergeant Moyano and his men explored the surrounding villages collecting tribute and prospecting for precious metals and gems. By the spring of 1567, Moyano had traveled into present-day

Tennessee where he made contact with the people of Chisca, a large town surrounded by a palisade wall. For some reason Moyano skirmished with these warriors and several of his men were wounded. At some point, as Spanish journals record, a Chisca chief sent a warning to Moyano, "If you return, I will kill you—and eat your dog!"[5] Evidently Moyano took this as a challenge not to be ignored and marched with fifteen men toward a Chisca town. In his letter to Pardo, the sergeant declared that his troops met the enemy, killed a thousand warriors and burned fifty houses. Fearing a counterattack, Moyano and his men found refuge nearby among the Chiaha, built a barricade and waited for Pardo to arrive with the army. Captain Pardo would not return until September to find his path to Mexico now blocked by hostile natives.

Pardo arrived in Joara on September 26, 1567. Shortly thereafter he journeyed west to rescue Moyano and by early October the expedition arrived at Chiaha where the people greeted Pardo as royalty and entertained with food, song and dance. In his journal, Pardo referred to this place as *tierra de angeles* (the land of angels). He remained there for almost two weeks before moving southwest toward Mexico. Along this route Pardo found Satapo where he was once again greeted as royalty; however, his request for food and native guides was never honored. Within a few days, Pardo noticed that there were no women or children in town and began to suspect that something was amiss. A soldier by the name of Alonso Velas came forward with a Satapo warrior who had a story to tell.

This warrior explained that five of his "brothers" once traveled as guides with other Spaniards (Soto in 1540) and these soldiers were attacked by the Coosa. His brothers were captured and enslaved. The Coosa, the man reported, and four other villages were now setting an ambush. Pardo retreated toward Joara by taking a roundabout trail, building and manning Fort San Pedro in Chiaha and Fort San Pablo to the east at Cauchi. Pardo arrived in Joara by early November and in a few weeks was on the trail again moving back to Guatari. By January 1568 Santa Elena sent another messenger requesting Pardo's return, once again, for fear of an attack from the French.

Pardo arrived at Santa Elena on March 2. Although he prepared for a French invasion that never came, Pardo was also planning to raise a larger army before returning to face the hostile natives of the "Blue Mountains." Within two months, however, the future of *La Florida* changed dramatically as word arrived in Santa Elena that a Native American uprising had occurred throughout the entire region. All forts had been attacked and burned, their defenders killed or missing. Thus ended the first chapter in the history of European attempts to colonize the backcountry of the Carolinas.

Lord John Carteret and the Granville Line

When North Carolina's General Assembly created Burke County in 1777 out of Rowan County, the charter decreed that Burke's southern boundary would follow the Granville Line at latitude 35° 34′ north, a boundary drawn early in the eighteenth century across this royal English colony of "Carolina" from the Atlantic coast to the "crest of the Blue Mountains." Much of this region was first recorded in a 1770 map by Captain John A. Collet, a surveyor from Switzerland. The original "Old Burke," therefore, included a vast area of northwestern North Carolina that ran into the yet to be state of Tennessee and would eventually give birth to all or part of seventeen new North Carolina counties.

A key player in this event, John Carteret, was born into a noble, aristocratic English family and obtained the title of Seigneur of Sark from 1715 to 1720, after which he sold the fiefdom and served King George II as ambassador to Sweden for over a decade. Upon his return to England, Lord Carteret became increasingly involved in English politics as a member of Parliament's House of Lords and at one point served as president of the king's council. With the death of his mother in 1744, he obtained the title Second Earl of Granville through his mother's father, Admiral Sir Richard Grenville.

Almost two hundred years before all this happened, one should remember that Sir Walter Raleigh's attempt in 1587 to establish an English colony on Roanoke Island failed. The first successful English colony was not founded until 1607 at Jamestown, Virginia, and the New England colony of Plymouth came years later in 1620. The English Crown at this time turned to wealthy aristocrats as a way to establish many more colonies before the Spanish and French took control of the New World.

In 1663 King Charles II awarded eight noblemen, including Lord Carteret's great-grandfather Sir George Carteret, a land grant for the American colony of Carolina. At this time Carolina stretched from Spanish Florida to Virginia and "west as far as the South Seas." Hoping to make

Lord John Carteret served England as ambassador to Sweden, member of the House of Lords and president of the King's Council. With the death of his mother in 1744, he obtained the title Second Earl of Granville, which became the name given to his property line across the colony of North Carolina. *Internet graphic. University of North Carolina-Chapel Hill Collection. 22 May 2007.*

a profit from silk and other crops in these temperate climates, these eight lord proprietors had to first entice settlers onto the land. Events moved more slowly in those days and it was not until 1670 that the lord proprietors actually colonized the area near present-day Charleston, South Carolina, to raise indigo and rice. During subsequent years, the northern section of Carolina around Pamlico Sound was actually occupied by an overflow of settlers from Virginia.

Due to lackluster profits from these colonies, plus problems with Native Americans and the colonist's increasing desire for provincial governors, the Crown decided in 1729 to buy out the lord proprietors to create the royal colonies of North Carolina and South Carolina. The southern part of South Carolina soon became Georgia (1732) under the proprietorship of James Oglethorpe and others. For various reasons, Lord Carteret retained his one-eighth inherited share but agreed to decline any participation in colonial government. His ownership was then restricted to a sixty-mile-wide section of land running east to west across North Carolina between the Virginia boundary and the Granville Line. Within his district, Lord Carteret sold land to all newcomers, including the Moravians at Salem, and deeded land to others such as gentleman John Perkins, in the yet to be named Burke County, for his services as a real estate guide in the frontier lands.

Upon his deathbed, friends insisted that Lord Carteret should rest but he insisted on reading a treaty draft that would end the French and Indian War in the colonies and the Seven Years' War in Europe. He remarked that nothing "could prolong my life to neglect my duty,"[6] and died at home on Arlington Street, London, January 22, 1763. The title of Second Earl of Granville descended to his son Robert, who died in 1776 just as the fever of "liberty" and the frustrations of "taxation without representation" caused a rebellion against the English Crown. The newly formed North Carolina General Assembly soon confiscated all royal lands, including Granville's district, following its "Halifax Resolves" in April and the signing of the Declaration of Independence in Philadelphia on July Fourth.

250-Year-Old Diary
Describes Old Burke

In the fall of 1752 Bishop Augustus Gottlieb Spangenberg of Switzerland traveled across the Catawba River Valley in search of land suitable for a new colony for the religious sect known as United Brethren (Moravian). He carefully recorded these experiences in a journal, the first known written account describing the flora, fauna and people of what one day would become Burke County, North Carolina. The United Brethren trace their beliefs to the teachings of John Hus, a thirteenth-century leader of the Czech-Bohemian-Moravia Reformation attempted within the Roman Catholic Church. Severely persecuted by surrounding Catholic armies, the Brethren almost disappeared. Not until after the Thirty Years' War (1618–1648), and with the protection of Nikolaus von Zinzendorf, a German Lutheran, did the United Brethren make a comeback.

Believing Scripture called all Christians to serve as God's missionaries of the Gospel, the Moravians became the first Protestant church to send missionaries into the non-Christian world. They evangelized among black slaves in the West Indies and the American colonies seeking to convert Native Americans to Christianity. With successful colonies already established in Georgia and Pennsylvania, Bishop Spangenberg sought a new colony in Carolina with a 100,000-acre land grant from Lord Proprietor John Carteret.

November 16: From camp on the Catawba River, about forty miles above A. Lambert's place...Our land lies in a region much frequented by the Catawbas, and Cherokees, especially for hunting. The Senecas too, came here almost every year, especially when they are at war with the Catawbas.[7]

Bishop Augustus Gottlieb Spangenberg of German Saxony began missionary work in 1735 with the establishment of a Moravian community in Pennsylvania. In 1752 Spangenberg was led across Burke County by local guide John Perkins but built Salem village in the piedmont at Winston-Salem. *Portrait line-drawing. N.C. Cultural Resources, Division of Archives and History.*

Spangenberg was born in German Saxony in 1704 and as a young man studied law before changing to theology and becoming a university professor. In 1735 he began missionary work in North America with the establishment of a Brethren community in Pennsylvania. Spangenberg was led inland to the Catawba River Valley by local trapper and guide John Perkins, who lived east of what is now Hickory. They found many rivers and streams with rich soil and a sparsely populated rugged landscape.

> *November 19: From camp on the middle river* [John's River]...*near Quaker Meadows, not far from Table Mountain...It lies seven or eight miles from the Catawba but the land between here and the mouth of the river is already taken up. I think we are near the Blue Mountains.*[8]

The earliest European settlers in the region included the Henry Weidner family from Pennsylvania, the Michaux family and a few Quaker missionaries living at "Quaker Meadows." Spangenberg's party continued seeking suitable space for a large village. At one point he wrote in the journal:

November 24: There's not much hardwood, mostly pine…There are many hunters here who work little, live like the Indians, shoot deer…From camp in the forks of the third river [Warrior Fork] *that flows into the Catawba near Quaker Meadows. Perhaps five miles from Table Mountain…This land is very rich, and has been much frequented by buffalo…The wolves here give us music every morning, from six corners at once.*[9]

Evidently there were no Native American villages in the region, since Spangenberg's journal only recorded sighting a few native hunters. We now know that Spaniards were actually the first Europeans to briefly visit this land—Hernando de Soto around 1540 and Captain Juan Pardo in 1567. History records that the diseases they left behind—smallpox, measles and typhoid—devastated native populations who had no resistance to these European germs. Archaeologists speculate that by the time Spangenberg arrived, fully half of all Native Americans in the region died from these plagues or moved away.

November 28: Old Indian Field, on the northeast branch [Caldwell County] *of Middle Little River…The Indians have certainly lived here, perhaps before the war with the white settlers in North Carolina. There are remains of an Indian Fort, grass still grows on the site of dwellings, and the trees show also that men have lived here, but it may be fifty or more years ago.*[10]

We must remember that Old Burke, at that time, was a true wilderness and the wild frontier of colonial settlement in North Carolina. Although these Moravians found a beautiful land during their travels here, evidently the wolves, Native Americans and "crowded" conditions of its bottomlands left much to be desired. Perkins, therefore, turned the Moravians north toward Watauga County, struggled over the massive mountains there and then turned east along the Yadkin River to find suitable land for a colony at Salem (Winston-Salem) in the piedmont. After this, Spangenberg made many trips between Europe and North America and on one voyage traveled with John Wesley, who, with his brother Charles, founded the Methodist Church in America. It is reported that their conversations during these many weeks of travel greatly influenced the Wesleys' commitment to "a religion of the heart" that seeks to spread the Gospel to all peoples. Spangenberg, during a later visit to America, officially established the Moravian Church of North America and within a few years returned to Germany where he remained a leader among Moravians until his death in 1792.

Who Named
Quaker Meadows?

It is interesting to think that as residents of Burke County we are exposed to history each day with the familiar names of places around us. First and foremost there is "Burke," named for an Irish hero of the American Revolution, Thomas Burke of Orange County, North Carolina. Then there's "Valdese" settled by Italian Waldensians in the 1890s, "Catawba" River for the American Indians who once lived along its banks and "Rutherford College" as home to our first college. But how did Quaker Meadows get its name—this rich, sandy bottomland along the Catawba River on North Green Street near Super K-Mart.

Just as other places are typically named for someone or something, should we not assume that these meadows were once home to Quakers? Founded as a Christian sect in seventeenth-century England by George Fox, the Society of Friends believed that an inner light of divine grace guided its followers without any special need for ritual, ceremony or clergy. With no music or preaching, monthly congregational meetings and annual regional gatherings could be very silent—or "quake" when the spirit of God moved the people.

Unlike their protestant brethren—Methodists, Lutherans, Baptists and Presbyterians—the Quakers did not structure their congregations into districts with authority vested in a national priesthood. In fact, Quakers denied the authority of all earthly empires and refused to swear allegiance to any king, to bear arms against another person, hold public office or pay tithes to the Church of England. This behavior sometimes brought persecution, fines and jail.

In order to escape this hell on earth, Quakers began to immigrate to the American colonies by the shipload. Their first settlements founded in New England were suspect to Puritans, who failed to accept these "undisciplined" Christians. Not until 1675 did Quakers find a safe haven when William Penn acquired a land grant to West Jersey. Pleased with Penn's accomplishments, King Charles II also granted him the colony of Pennsylvania in 1681. Another region that attracted Quakers was the eastern and piedmont sections of the Carolina colony. Church records indicate that meetinghouses of the Society of Friends were established in Perquimans County, North Carolina, as early as 1681. In following decades, other Quaker settlements were located in Alamance and Guilford counties, which remain a stronghold of the faith today.

The lure of cheap and sometimes free land during the eighteenth century attracted thousands of other settlers into the Carolina piedmont from northern colonies and resulted in North Carolina's population doubling between 1732 and 1754. Many of these early pioneers were Pennsylvania "Dutch" Germans, Scots, Irish and recent English immigrants looking to avoid the "crowded lands" along the Atlantic coast. Could some of these new Carolinians have been Quaker?

The earliest pioneers arrived in the vicinity of present-day Burke County before 1750 as the Henry Weidner (Whitner) family from Pennsylvania settled on Henry River and the Michaux family resided along what later became known as John's River. As a young man, John Perkins received a grant of land from the English Earl of Granville in payment for his services as a guide to Bishop Spangenberg's (Moravian) survey of the upper Catawba River. It is because of this particular visit that we have the first written mention of "Quakers." On November 24, 1752, Spangenberg wrote: "From camp in the forks of the third river [Warrior Fork] that flows into the Catawba near Quaker Meadows. Perhaps five miles from Table Mountain." He makes no further comment about these Quakers, and seemingly, neither has anyone else.

What we may surmise from these tantalizing bits of information is that Quakers were indeed in Burke County before 1752, and perhaps a decade earlier. These Quakers may have escaped the Puritans of New England and fled to Old Burke, or more likely they came from North Carolina colonies farther east. At best, our Quakers numbered nothing more than a few families, but they were here long enough for others to call their settlement "Quaker Meadows." It's also logical to think that the missionary calling of the Society of Friends would have specifically placed them in Old Burke (a wild frontier at that time) to save the souls of Native Americans. Evidently, our Quaker friends were gone soon after 1752, perhaps scared off by raiding Cherokee warriors encouraged by the French during the French and Indian Wars of 1753–1763.

Quaker Meadows
Presbyterian Church

Religion and churches have always been an important part of living in Burke County. "Revivals," "camp meetings" and "homecomings" continue to be seen today among our churches—but just how many activities can a church squeeze into its annual homecoming event? Little Quaker Meadows Presbyterian Church, north on highway 181 and mother church to First Presbyterian of Morganton, provides a model for others to follow. Pastor Andy Parkey and many members of the congregation worked for weeks to make this August 28, 2004 homecoming extra special.

As the first organized denominational church in Burke County, founded prior to 1777 by Scots and Irish who arrived on the frontier of this English Carolina colony, the congregation has held many homecomings, but this time was different—beginning with the morning worship service. Reverend Richard Morgan, who served as a recent interim pastor, returned from his new home in Pennsylvania to deliver the sermon, "Homecoming Now and Then," which reflected upon this church and all past congregations as "members of the household of God." Dr. Morgan is author of *Founded On the Rock: A History of Quaker Meadows Presbyterian Church* that was published last year.

In an earlier book, Judge Alphonso C. Avery reported that Reverend James Templeton, who is the first known pastor at Quaker Meadows, also served at Pleasant Garden and Ready Branch. Templeton is also likely the first minister to speak about organizing a Presbyterian church in Morganton (i.e. organized prior to 1797). Synod records indicate that he spoke at a meeting of Presbytery April 2, 1784.[11] This was the same year that "Morgan's Town," named for General Daniel Morgan, became the county seat. While the first Presbyterian Synod in the South was created in 1770, the Synod of the Carolinas was not founded until 1788.

Founded before 1777, Quaker Meadows Presbyterian is the first organized denominational church in Burke with Pastor James Templeton. Most likely, he is the person who also helped organize the First Presbyterian Church of Morganton sometime prior to 1797, which then shared its building with several other denominations. *Author Collection.*

And what would a homecoming be without a covered dish dinner on the grounds? Following worship everyone gathered at nearby picnic tables to partake of good, wholesome, homecooked food prepared by some of the best "chefs" in the county. At some point, local photographer John Payne created an old-fashioned panoramic picture of all those present. Later in the afternoon the Penland Historical Society held its family reunion in honor of their ancestor Robert Penland, a founder and first elder of Quaker Meadows Presbyterian Church. As many as one hundred Penland descendants attended from various states across the nation. You see, genealogy and church history go hand in hand around Burke County.

Robert Penland married Elizabeth Brank and together they raised ten children along Canoe Creek at present-day Whisnant Road in the Oak Hill community. Robert died in 1828 at eighty-four years of age. Elizabeth died in 1841 at the age of ninety-five. Both are buried in the family cemetery located at Frank Whisnant Road on property now owned by the Ora Lee Carswell family. During the American War for Independence, Robert served with Colonel McDowell and fought in battles at Ramsour's Mill and Kings Mountain. In honor of Robert's service to his country, his descendants dedicated a U.S. military marker to their forefather in the church's Bost Memorial Garden.

Roscoe White of Charlotte, coordinator of the Penland family reunion, scheduled a very special event to end this most special homecoming day—a wedding between himself and Donna Musslewhite of Monroe. As a seventh generation descendant of Robert Penland, White said, "I could think of no better time to have a wedding than during the homecoming at Quaker Meadows."[12] The Whites honeymooned in Morganton before continuing on to Asheville. Somehow history, family, good food, Christian fellowship and love all seem to fit together at a church's homecoming.

Kings Mountain Battle Has Deep Roots in Burke

Burke County was founded by North Carolina's new General Assembly in the midst of war as American colonists fought for freedom from the British Crown. In that year of 1777, "Old Burke" included all of northwestern North Carolina and was sparsely populated with mostly English, Scottish and Irish farmers in a few wilderness settlements. There was neither a town nor courthouse. In fact, the little village of Elder's Spring would not be listed in the state until 1785 as the county seat at Morgan's Town.

The first battles of the Revolution in our region actually began in 1776 as Cherokee warriors, encouraged by the British, attacked settlers along the western frontier. In response, General Griffith Rutherford of Salisbury led an expedition against the Cherokee to destroy their towns. This "Cherokee problem," however, would not end for Burke County until 1790 when the American Indian territory was moved farther west into the Appalachian Mountains.

As the major battles of the American Revolution shifted from Northern colonies to the South, Charleston fell to the British and General Cornwallis led his troops through South Carolina on a bloody rampage toward Charlotte, North Carolina. Major Patrick Ferguson's orders were to protect Cornwallis's left flank, rally loyal Tories in the Carolinas' backcountry and encourage the Cherokee to continue their attacks on "rebel" settlements. Perhaps the first fight in Old Burke against British regulars occurred during September 1780 when Major Ferguson surprised Colonel Charles McDowell's small band of Patriots at the head of Cane Creek near Brindletown. His brother, Major Joseph McDowell, also entered the fray and together these Burke rebels fought the British to a draw.

Following this battle, the McDowells retreated northward over the mountains into the Watauga settlements where the "Over Mountain Men" learned they

In September of 1780 some 1,400 Patriots gathered at Quaker Meadows to plan an attack on British forces. The leaders met beneath the "Council Oak" to discuss strategy. On the next day they began their march into history and victory at Kings Mountain. *Internet graphic (1889). Photographer unknown. U.S. Park Service "Kings Mountain National Battleground." 14 November 2006.*

This federal-style brick plantation house was built in 1812 by Captain Charles McDowell Jr. at Quaker Meadows. Open to the public as a historic site, the property was deeded to the Historic Burke Foundation in 1986 by Duke Power/Crescent Land and Timber Corporation. *Author Collection.*

must leave their homes and families to stop Ferguson before he plundered their region. Major Ferguson was already on the move in search of food for his troops, traveling as far north as Buck Creek (present-day McDowell County). Ferguson then marched south to camp in Gilbert Town (Rutherfordton) at about the same time the McDowell brothers were returning to their father's homestead at Quaker Meadows (Morganton). Isaac Shelby and John Sevier soon followed from the Watauga and Nolachucky settlements (northeast Tennessee) to gather an additional four hundred men at Sycamore Shoals.

Colonel Cleveland (Wilkes County) and Joseph Winston (Surry County) were already on the trail, passing Crider's Fort (Lenior) before crossing Lovelady's Ford on the Catawba River. By September 30, 1780, almost

Kings Mountain Battle Has Deep Roots in Burke

1,400 Patriots were camped in the McDowell fields at Quaker Meadows. The McDowells shared their food stores and allowed the men to burn fence rails for cooking and warmth. The following day, all the "colonels" held council beneath a magnificent oak tree and planned their attack on Major Ferguson at Gilbert Town. This is the famous "Council Oak" of local fame. Eventually, Colonel William Campbell of Virginia was elected to command this band of "barbarians" (as Ferguson named them). Major Joseph McDowell would lead the Burke troops while his brother Charles traveled to Hillsborough to report their plans to General Gates.

Various scrimmages with Tories and British troops followed as these 1,400 Over Mountain Men spread out and moved south in search of Ferguson. Realizing that he may be outnumbered, Ferguson moved his troops west to Kings Mountain (South Carolina) and sent couriers to Cornwallis requesting reinforcements. Standing atop this small hill, only some sixty feet high, Ferguson (the only British soldier present) decided to stand his ground with almost one thousand locally recruited Tories. Soon thereafter, Colonel Campbell arrived with his Over Mountain Men to join South Carolina and Georgia Patriots in surrounding Kings Mountain with nearly two thousand men. The battle on October 7, 1780, was brief—perhaps an hour. It ended with Major Ferguson dead along with two hundred Loyalists. Colonel Campbell reported twenty-eight American dead and sixty-two wounded.

In his 1881 book, *Kings Mountain and Its Heroes*, Lyman Draper indicates that Captain Joseph McDowell of Pleasant Garden appropriated Ferguson's table china while Colonel Shelby acquired Ferguson's silver whistle. Captain Sevier is reported to have taken the British officer's silk sash and sword. This ignoble defeat at Kings Mountain had, in fact, changed the course of British military strategy in the South, and therefore contributed to Cornwallis's surrender at Yorktown the following year.

Today, we have many Burke Countians to thank for preserving this significant moment in our history and its memories: the North Carolina Room at the Burke Public Library for protecting these eighteenth-century records, the Burke County Genealogical Society for preserving the family histories of these Patriots, the Historical Society of Burke County for its annual speakers forum, the Historic Burke Foundation for restoring Charles McDowell's house at Quaker Meadows, the Daughters of the American Revolution for a plaque that commemorates the brave Over Mountain Men meeting at Quaker Meadows and the History Museum of Burke County for adopting the Council Oak as their symbol to forever remind us of this sacrifice for freedom at the 1780 Battle of Kings Mountain.

General Daniel Morgan
American Hero at Cowpens

Fourth of July 2004 was a great one, again, especially since I was able to join our local Table Rock Shooters pyrotechnics team in "painting the night sky in colors." Celebrating our nation's birthday is always exciting to me, but playing with Zambelli fireworks at the same time is the best. Table Rock Shooters had six shows over two days with sparkling success as thousands of shells were launched into the heavens. Breathing acrid smoke, enduring hot sparks and dodging exploding shells are all part of an evening's work for these fellows. For me, working as a helper at Cowpens, South Carolina, turned into a memorable evening.

Yes, friends, there is a small town just across the state line named Cowpens, which in colonial times served as a crossroads stockyard. But more importantly, a very significant battle of the American Revolution took place there in 1781 as Brigadier General Daniel Morgan, the town of Morganton's namesake, challenged the seemingly unbeatable British lieutenant colonel, Banastre Tarleton.

After passing through the entrance to Cowpens National Battlefield, the fireworks team was directed to a small area some distance from the visitor's center where Morgan formed his first battle line across Green River Road. As I stepped out of the truck onto this hallowed ground, I tried to imagine that January day long ago when the fate of a young republic hung in the balance. This landscape is flat for the piedmont, with a large pasture surrounded by a grove of oak trees. With 1,200 troops, Morgan placed mostly sharpshooters on the front line to take out British field officers and hopefully "Bloody Tarleton" himself, the man given credit for a recent slaughter of captured American Patriots. Behind these riflemen stood untrained Carolina and Georgia militiamen under the command of South Carolina's Andrew Pickens.

Daniel Morgan was a rough and tumble wagon driver in Virginia before his riflemen joined the American Revolution battles at Quebec and Saratoga. General Morgan later won a decisive victory over British regulars at Cowpens, South Carolina. The city of Morganton is his namesake. *Portrait by Charles Wilson Peale. Internet graphic. City of Philadelphia. 22 May 2007.*

We began to unload the mortar tubes, positioning the racks east to west across Green River Road. This fireworks show included six-, five-, four- and three-inch aerial shells with Asian names for red blooming chrysanthemum, silver spider web with tiger tail and blue rose with titanium salute. Unlike that winter day some two hundred years ago, we worked in the humid afternoon of a hot summer sun. I thought I heard men moving among the trees. A second American line was being formed by Captain John

Howard with veteran Continental troops from Maryland and Virginia. William Washington, a cousin of General Washington, protected the rear with 350 cavalry. Knowing that he was facing a well-trained and combat-ready army, Morgan's strategy was to have each line, especially the front comprised mostly of farmers and men from the Blue Ridge hills, fire several volleys and then retreat back to the next line. This strategy later served Continental General Greene well at the Battle of Guilford Courthouse in North Carolina.

At various moments I heard the shuffle of foot soldiers moving among the trees around Cowpens, the quiet chatter of Patriots as they rammed powder and ball into their muskets. A few horses neighed in the background as Tarleton rode into view, his 1,200 redcoats marching in step and his legion cavalry circling to the left. Our Table Rock pyrotechnicians loaded more than six hundred shells that day with almost one-third exploding during a dramatic finale. As the stage band at the visitor's center played Sousa marches, we hustled to finish. It was getting dark fast in this flat country. The shooters lit their flares. We were ready. As our first shells climbed high into the sky, we could hear the music rise louder and the crowd yell.

British cavalry charged the American line as their two cannons pounded Morgan's two thousand troops. American sharpshooters fired volley after volley, killing two-thirds of Tarleton's officers, and then retreated into the Continental line. Tarleton sent his dragoons in chase with fixed bayonets. The entire British force charged forward and engaged in furious hand-to-hand combat. Fire and brimstone rained down upon the fireworks crew. The smell of sulfur was heavy in the air and the thick smoke from burning shells made it difficult to breathe. The sound was deafening. Sweat and gunpowder mixed to blind our eyes. I thought I heard the scream of men and horses. Pickens's militia formed a new line and fired into the British left. Washington's cavalry rode into battle. Morgan and Howard regrouped the Continentals and militia into a new front at the rear. Mixed with these death cries and the screams of wounded were the curses of men in battle.

Within the seconds and minutes of one hour, the British attack collapsed. Tarleton fled the field leaving one hundred dead, two hundred wounded and six hundred prisoners to the Americans. Following the recent defeat of British Major Patrick Ferguson and Loyalists at Kings Mountain, this victory was another nail in the coffin of Lord Cornwallis's grand army. We lit the show's finale. It was stupendous! Ka-boom! Ka-boom! Ka-boom! Over two hundred rockets raced into the darkness to explode among the stars. An appropriate salute, I thought, to those brave American Patriots who fought and spilled their blood on this field to win the battle of Cowpens.

Thomas Burke
Statesman and Patriot

If you ask someone around here for whom Burke County was named you may hear "Sir Edmund Burke" or some other "Burke," and then sometimes you might hear the correct response: "Thomas Burke." Little else is known of this man for whom Burke County was named.

"Old Burke" is often the local reference to the one created by the state's first elected General Assembly on June 1, 1777, out of a divided Rowan County. Back then, the boundaries encompassed much of northwestern North Carolina and, therefore, exhibited little resemblance to the Burke County we see today on maps. It's also important to remember that the county of Burke was born in the midst of revolution only two years after American colonial Patriots fired "the shot heard around the world" in Massachusetts. This epic struggle with King George of England would not end until eight years later with a treaty signed in Paris.

Dr. Thomas Burke, very much the Catholic Irishman, became an eloquent spokesman for rebellion against the British. He immigrated to the colonies from Ireland in the 1760s and briefly practiced medicine (most likely midwifery) in Virginia before arriving in Orange County, North Carolina, around 1772. There he practiced law and became very much involved in local politics.

In those days, a key issue that moved North Carolina into the forefront of revolution was a disagreement between the royal governor and the colonial legislature over the right of local courts to exercise judicial authority. As the word "liberty" began to creep across the colonies, North Carolina followed Virginia's lead in establishing anti-British committees of correspondence throughout the region to keep people informed about current issues. Later, as news of the Boston Tea Party arrived, these Patriots called for a meeting at New Bern to discuss British colonial policies. Thomas Burke served as a representative during the extralegal provincial congresses held at New Bern,

Thomas Burke immigrated to the colonies from Ireland in the 1760s and briefly lived in Virginia before arriving in Orange County, North Carolina, ca.1772. There he practiced law and became involved in local politics and the call for independence from King George and the British Empire. Burke County is his namesake. *Internet graphic. Friends of Ulster-USA. 22 May 2007.*

Hillsborough and Halifax between 1774 and 1776. The Halifax Resolves of April 12, 1776, are recorded in history as the first official act by a colony to speak of independence from the British Empire.

During the state's general elections that followed, Thomas Burke was elected as a representative to a fifth provincial congress to draft a new state constitution. In these debates he was on the side of moderation and opposed a strong executive governor. This view prevailed and North Carolina's constitution made a broad commitment to representative government with a bill of rights and universal voting for all property owners. During the first General Assembly session in 1777, Thomas Burke was appointed as one of three delegates to America's Continental Congress in Philadelphia and, most likely, had his name mentioned for one of the new North Carolina counties. At the Philadelphia debates, he supported the development of a simple union of the states and the ratification of America's first republican government under the Articles of Confederation.

Following his return to North Carolina in early 1781, which was during the War for Independence, Burke was elected our third governor. In a matter of months, however, he was captured by a local band of British Loyalists and ultimately imprisoned on Sullivan's Island near Charleston. Once "paroled" by the British with a promise to not support the rebellion, Burke returned to the governor's chair to complete his one-year term. There followed a series of successful Patriot battles against the British at Kings Mountain, Cowpens and Guilford Courthouse before the final surrender of Lord Cornwallis at Yorktown in 1781. Only then could Thomas Burke finally leave politics and return to farming on his Tyaquin Plantation near Hillsborough.

Waightstill Avery
Patriot and Gentleman

During the eighteenth century, the Avery family was among the outstanding pioneer families of colonial North Carolina. This famous lineage began with the arrival of Waightstill Avery to eastern North Carolina in 1769. Avery was born in Connecticut into a prominent English family and was a graduate with honors from Princeton.

Having first served in the colonial provincial assembly and later as attorney general for the Crown, Avery resigned both positions in the early 1770s and began supporting the American cause for local governance and independence from the British Empire. During the war that followed, Colonel Avery bought Swans Pond Plantation along the Catawba River in Burke County, sent his family to this distant frontier and led the Jones County militia into battle. His greatest contribution to the war effort, however, continued to be his insight into the political and legal issues required for independence.

Avery served on the committee that drafted the Mecklenburg Resolves (1775), which declared English law to be "null and vacated" and thus required new laws to govern an independent nation. During the next year he worked with others on a draft of North Carolina's first constitution, evidently as secretary, since the copy now at the state archives in Raleigh is mostly transcribed in Avery's handwriting. He was then elected to the first freely elected North Carolina General Assembly in 1777 and named the state's first attorney general.

Within a few years the major battles of the American Revolution shifted from the Northern colonies to the South. Charleston fell to the British and Lord Cornwallis marched his twelve-thousand-man army through South Carolina toward Charlotte, the Mecklenburg County then known as the "Hornets Nest" of rebellion. Major Patrick Ferguson protected

Swan Pond Plantation, as seen today along the Catawba River, was acquired by Waightstill Avery in 1778, Patriot of the Revolution and first attorney general of North Carolina. He acquired thousands of acres across Old Burke and his relatives continue to live on the family farm today. *Author Collection*.

Cornwallis's left flank, sought loyal Tories in the Carolina backcountry and encouraged Cherokee raids along the frontier. The defeat of Ferguson at Kings Mountain in 1780, the defeat of Lieutenant Colonel Tarleton at Cowpens in 1781 and, soon thereafter, the defeat of Cornwallis at Guilford Courthouse contributed to the British surrender at Yorktown.

After the war, Avery's Swan Pond Plantation prospered along with his family and he became much involved in acquiring land throughout Old Burke. Avery returned to the practice of law, typically appearing in court dressed in colonial knee breeches and powdered wig. With his knowledge of law and deft arguments at court, Avery attracted a sizable following with one such admirer being a young man named Andrew Jackson of Tennessee and a future president of the United States. Jackson had earlier asked Avery to tutor him in the law but Avery rejected the request due to a "lack of accommodations." The young, spirited twenty-one-year-old Jackson then chose to complete his studies with a lawyer in Salisbury and eventually moved to Jonesboro, Tennessee.

In 1788 the two men found themselves in court on opposing sides. At some point in this trial, Avery's rhetoric, barbs and wit embarrassed Jackson, which caused an exchange of accusations that resulted in Jackson challenging Avery to a duel. Avery accepted. With no desire to shed blood, both met on the field of honor the next day and promptly fired their guns into the air. Luckily for everyone involved—and the nation—the duel was over.

By the beginning of the nineteenth century Waightstill Avery had accumulated large tracts of land throughout western North Carolina, including some thirteen thousand acres in Burke County. Nearby Avery County, just northwest of Burke, is named in his honor. Over the coming years Avery's descendants became active in agriculture, law, business and state and local politics. His only surviving son, Isaac Thomas Avery, acquired more than fifty thousand acres in Mitchell and Avery counties where he raised more cattle and horses than anyone in western North Carolina.

By 1850, Isaac Thomas also owned 140 slaves and several gold mines in Burke and Rutherford counties. During the War Between the States, five of his sons fought for the Confederacy but only one, Alphonso Calhoun Avery, survived. Isaac Erwin, who led two regiments against the Yankees at Cemetery Hill in the Battle of Gettysburg, fell fatally wounded in the neck and sent a last message home: "Major, tell my father I died with my face to the enemy."[13]

The Avery family looms large in both North Carolina and Burke County history and it is a shame that no image or painting seems to exist of its progenitor and North Carolina's first attorney general, Waightstill Avery. The closest likeness is, perhaps, a photograph of his grandson William. Should someone find Waightstill's likeness, please call the *News Herald*.

The State of Franklin Secedes from Old Burke

The American colonies' fight with the British ended on September 3, 1783, with the Treaty of Paris. By its terms, Britain recognized the independence of the United States of America with boundaries that now extended west to the Mississippi River. Spain, a cosigner, agreed to open navigation from New Orleans on the Mississippi and Gulf of Mexico. With this treaty, North Carolina acquired millions of new acres of land west of the Appalachian Mountains. On this new frontier, Burke was North Carolina's westernmost judicial district, and therefore ever so briefly held jurisdiction over those new adjacent mountain areas that included the Allegheny region near the Virginia line.

This is where the Watauga Association had existed since 1772. These settlers, against British policy at that time, had crossed the Allegheny Mountains from Virginia to live on Cherokee lands. Finding themselves beyond Crown authority, they formed the Watauga Association, elected officials and began to govern themselves. When the Treaty of Paris was signed, the Watauga settlements were scattered along the Cumberland River toward present-day Nashville and in 1784 North Carolina decided to give this region to the Continental Congress as payment of its war debt. The Watauga settlers, upset with this idea, began to argue against the plan. North Carolina's General Assembly, fearing it had acted in haste, rescinded its offer to Congress and created several new counties in the region (today northeast Tennessee).

North Carolina also ordered the establishment of courts, the enrollment of a militia brigade to enforce its laws and appointed John Sevier, a hero at the Battle of Kings Mountain, as militia commander. On August 23, 1784, delegates from four of the newly created counties met at Jonesborough to declare their independence from North Carolina and in the next year

The Birthright, a locally produced outdoor play written by Maude Patton Anthony, was presented in the early 1920s on the N.C. School for the Deaf campus. Its actors depicted the Goddess of Liberty and Father Time in a dramatic tale of Burke County during the Revolution. *Burke County Public Library, Picture Burke Collection.*

Fourth of July celebrations continue to be a favorite event for Burke Countians with parades, speeches and picnics seen in most communities. Fireworks are a must, and over the past two decades aerial displays have been provided by a local group of volunteers known as the Table Rock Shooters. *Burke County Public Library, Picture Burke Collection.*

petitioned Congress to be admitted as "the state of Franklin." As a footnote to this story, Benjamin Franklin refused to support their request. Under the U.S. Articles of Confederation, a two-thirds vote in favor was required in Congress, but this magic number was not reached and the Watauga Association decided on another tactic.

Soon thereafter, they drafted a constitution for a new state modeled after North Carolina's, held elections and set the first legislative meeting for

December 1785 in Greeneville. John Sevier, now nicknamed "Nolichucky Jack," was elected governor and the free and independent State of Franklin was born, albeit illegally. Taxes and salaries were fixed and payable with money or bartered goods and Governor Sevier received some pay in deerhides. This precarious situation lasted less than three years as North Carolina reestablished its sovereignty in the region with a state militia under the command of John Tipton. The only battle between the two governments occurred in 1788 as Tipton was ordered to seize Sevier's estate for treason, since he had recently contacted the Spanish consul in Washington with a request for military support.

Tipton's troops captured Sevier's two sons, but John escaped into Native American country, although the Cherokee had been waging a furious war against the Watauga settlements for years. Months thereafter Sevier commanded a renegade band of settlers who attacked and burned Cherokee towns. On one occasion, a young man bereaved over the death of his family at the hands of Cherokee warriors, bludgeoned several chiefs under Sevier's protection. When this news reached North Carolina, a new warrant was issued for John Sevier's arrest for violating Indian Territory.

While visiting friends in Jonesborough, Sevier was surprised by Tipton and taken prisoner to be trotted off in irons to the nearest court at Morganton in Burke County. Sheriff William Morrison accepted the prisoner but soon released him into the custody of Generals Joseph and Charles McDowell, local Revolutionary War heroes. While awaiting trial, Sevier's two sons arrived in Morganton to mix with the huge crowds gathered to witness this extraordinary event. At some point in the days that followed, John Sevier and his sons made their escape from Burke County and returned to friends in the isolated Allegheny hills. In order to end this disagreement, North Carolina agreed to drop all charges if Sevier would swear allegiance to the State of North Carolina.

John Sevier did swear and was soon elected as Washington County's state senator to North Carolina's General Assembly. Following adoption of the U.S. Constitution in 1789, Sevier was elected as a North Carolina congressman to the first U.S. House of Representatives. After this, in 1796, he became the first governor of the State of Tennessee. Following two terms as governor, Sevier then served in Tennessee's Senate and in 1811 was reelected to the U.S. House of Representatives. Sevier died in 1815.

André Michaux Slept Here

He really did—but it was over two hundred years ago. André Michaux (pronounced Mish-aw), the world famous French botanist, actually made a stopover in Burke County during his world travels to study the plants in our area. You may have noticed the historic highway marker near Burger King at Quaker Meadows recording his stay on the nights of September 8, 1794, and May 2, 1795, at Swan Ponds with the Waightstill Avery family.

Prior to visiting the young United States of America, Michaux traveled throughout Europe collecting seeds and plants for further study back home. Although left for dead by bandits in Persia, Michaux recovered, returned to Paris with the mimosa, ginkgo and camellia—and a French-Persian dictionary that he compiled while recovering from his injuries. Evidently, these adventures came from grief following the death of his wife during childbirth.

Michaux's fame as a botanist gained the attention of the king's royal gardener who asked him to explore America in search of "useful trees." At that time France was rapidly depleting its forest and the need for shipbuilding lumber was rapidly increasing. Michaux arrived in New York City in 1785 with his teenage son, François, and a couple of helpers. Almost immediately he established a garden along the Hudson River and began to send specimens to France. A short time later he created a similar research garden in Charleston, South Carolina. The French soon learned of the American magnolia, cypress (great for building ships), sweet potato and cranberry.

For over a decade André Michaux walked and rode horseback among the Atlantic states, traveled into the backwoods of the Appalachian frontier, ventured into Indian Territory and ultimately as far west as the Great

Frenchman André Michaux traveled the world in search of useful plants and then, as a botanist for King Louis XVI, arrived in America in 1785. By the fall of 1794 he came into Burke County to study mountain flora and visit with Waightstill Avery at Swan Ponds. Reenactor Charles Williams portrays Michaux before students visiting the History Museum of Burke County. *Author Collection.*

Plains. On most occasions his was the first scientific study and naming of native American flora. At home, the French became familiar with *Mirabilia nyctaginea* (wild four-o'clock), *Salix caroliniana* (Carolina willow), *Habenaria guingueseta* (creeping orchid) and hundreds of unique plants of the southern Appalachians—some of which are only found here and in Asia.

At some point he traveled into western North Carolina, collected over 2,500 specimens, stood atop Black Dome (later known as Mount Mitchell) and named the local mountain range *Montagnes Noires*, the "Black Mountains." Michaux shared his excitement with American scientists and even met George Washington and Benjamin Franklin. Injury and disease did not slow this man down, nor did the French Revolution, which removed King Louis XVI and established a republic in France. In 1793, Michaux spoke with President Thomas Jefferson about a grand botanical expedition to the Pacific coast but Congress did not get around to funding this idea until after Michaux returned home. That historic journey would eventually become known as the Lewis and Clark expedition. The following year, while in Charleston recovering from another bout with malaria, he made plans to return to the southern Appalachian Mountains.

This expedition took him along the banks of the Wateree, Santee and Catawba rivers into North Carolina, near the current location of the Daniel Stowe Botanical Garden on Lake Wylie with its André Michaux Nature Trail. This is most likely the same path followed by Spaniards Hernando de Soto (1541) and Juan Pardo (1566) over two centuries earlier. The *Magnolia macrophylla* (bigleaf magnolia) and the *Rhododendron catawbiense* (Catawba rhododendron) received their names during this late summer trip.

Apparently Michaux had his first sleepover at Swan Ponds in Burke County after visiting the high mountains of northwest North Carolina. On August 28, 1794, he climbed to the top of Grandfather Mountain for an awesome, panoramic view of green grandeur, a botanical paradise. His diary records the moment and his great passion: "I sang the Marseillaise and shouted, 'Long live America and the Republic of France!'"[14] In nearby hills and valleys he discovered the flaming azalea, lily of the valley and mountain laurel. His name will always be associated with *Malus angustifolia Michaux* and *Ranuculus hispidus Michaux*.

After his September stay in Burke County, Michaux again climbed into the high hill country toward Roan Mountain to follow the Avery Trace into Tennessee. From there he moved on to Nashville and later Kentucky, returning to Charleston a year later. On his return voyage to Paris in 1798, Michaux almost died when his ship wrecked in a storm off the coast of Holland. Only good luck allowed him to salvage most of his specimens and notebooks. A few years after this, he succumbed to fever while collecting his beloved seeds and plants on an expedition off the coast of Africa in Madagascar.

André Michaux is known among the world's scientists as a great explorer, botanist and scholar—and also for naming over twenty genera and almost three hundred species of flowering plants in North America. It's even possible that the giant bald cypress growing at Swan Ponds today was his gift to Waightstill Avery. Had Michaux been American, I am certain that we would remember him as a national hero. As a visitor to Burke County, we feel honored to have had, once upon a time, such a distinguished guest in our midst.

There's Gold in Them Th'r Hills

The first certified gold mine in the United States (1792) was the Reed Gold Mine in Cabarrus County, North Carolina. With gold mining you need a foundry to process raw gold into coins or bullion. Christopher Bechtler's private mint in Rutherford County, North Carolina, produced the first gold dollar in the United States. During the peak of this North Carolina Gold Rush from 1830–1850, some fifty-six mines were in operation across the state with more than twelve thousand miners working its creeks and streams.

Burke County contributed greatly to the spread of "gold fever" during this time. In 1828 gold was discovered, quite by accident, in Brindle Creek at the foot of Pilot Mountain in southern Burke. It seems that a certain Samuel Martin of Connecticut was on his way home after an unsuccessful adventure into the gold mines of South America. Footsore from worn-out shoes, Martin came upon the log home of Bob Anderson where the promise of a quarter would get supper, a night's sleep and repaired shoes.

While walking around the Anderson cabin, a bee sting on the hand caused Martin to jerk away and scrape his knuckles against the house. The sight of blood caused Martin to look closely at the logs, and to his surprise, he found a large gold nugget stuck in the clay chinking. The rest of the story, as they say, is history. Over the next several months, partners Anderson and Martin panned gold out of Brindle Creek and split their findings fifty-fifty. Samuel Martin rode out of Burke County with $20,000 in gold while Bob Anderson, within a few years, lost his land to Joseph McDowell Carson.

This man, and other Burke plantation owners, brought in heavy equipment and slaves to build mines and to do the dirty work. Gold fever eventually reached far and wide to attract out-of-state investors who brought hundreds of workers into the South Mountains of Burke County. Reports indicate

The Henderson gristmill operated in northern Burke County for over fifty years along Upper Creek. During the nineteenth century most communities had a water powered mill nearby to grind corn or wheat. Steam powered mills appeared early in the next century. *H. Eugene Willard.* Images of America: Morganton and Burke County. *Charleston: Arcadia Press, 2001.*

that a typical mine could bring in over $2,000 each week. Colonel Walton remarked that $30,000 worth of gold was "taken from not as much as an acre of land at Jamestown by Col. Joseph Erwin and W.F. McKesson."[15] Erwin was a prominent local landowner while McKesson invested in timber and logging companies. Hundreds of prospectors, however, found far less gold by panning in creeks and streams.

The South Mountain Belt is a large gold-bearing region throughout Burke, McDowell and Rutherford counties, extending east toward Gastonia and Charlotte. North Carolina led the nation in gold production in those early years with an estimated 1830s value of over $1 million ($10 million today) per year until the 1848 California Gold Rush. Raw gold is not as useful as coined money and these early miners and "panners" had nowhere to send their gold to be minted. The U.S. mint at Philadelphia did not stamp its first coin until 1849, while the private Charlotte Mint produced coins after 1835. Before that date, and for another twenty-five years, the mint of Christopher Bechtler of Rutherfordton (1831) served Burke miners and the region. It is estimated that the Bechtlers handled over $250,000 in gold each year during this gold rush.

"Bechtler gold" was so well known for its pure content that it became the preferred coinage ($5, $2.50 and $1) during the War Between the States and the most common of all gold pieces found among westward bound pioneers. Christopher Bechtler, followed by his son August, produced twenty-nine varieties of gold coins, but no known collection exists with a complete set. The North Carolina Museum of History in Raleigh perhaps has the best Bechtler collection anywhere.

As the California Gold Rush overshadowed the North Carolina mines, gold fever continued to infect a few hardy Burke citizens with wanderlust, and eventually hundreds packed their bags and headed to California by horse, wagon, or if they had the money, by steamship out of Charleston. One report tells of twenty-five men departing Burke County in 1852, half of these being slaves with their owners. This group sailed out of Charleston, crossed the Isthmus of Panama by land and then sailed on to California. A few died from "Panama fever" but the others reached the western gold fields to collect $5–$10 per day. A few brief years later, the War Between the States ended most Burke County discussions about gold. The surface gold and "branch gold" across the county was becoming increasingly difficult to find. A few mines continued to operate but the "gold fever" of the 1830s and 1840s was gone.

As I stand on my porch looking at Table Rock a thought comes to mind, "There's gold in them th'r hills!" And as I scan nearby Irish Creek, I just wonder: Does Smokefoot Trade Company in downtown Morganton still have that gold panning stuff?

Confederate Training Camp Destroyed

I recently read in the *News Herald* that the N.C. Division of Tourism is creating a Civil War Trail across the state as part of a national historic trails system. Although Burke's marker only recognizes Union Major General George Stoneman's raid in 1865, there was an earlier, equally devastating Yankee attack the year before.

Before daylight on June 28, 1864, some two hundred Union soldiers walked silently through thick Burke County woods several miles east of Morganton. Under command of Captain G.W. Kirk, they had traveled from Tennessee weeks earlier to plunder Confederate towns in northwestern North Carolina. Most of his men carried the new repeating Spencer rifle, which in effect doubled their firepower. Some of the raiders were North Carolina recruits. Some were American Indians. Ahead was Camp Vance, a tiny village of barracks for conscripted troops and a few cabins and storage sheds. A small hospital and icehouse were situated west of the camp. Speagle's Turnout was also nearby, the end of the line for the state's Western North Carolina Rail Road.

The Union soldiers encircled the camp and waited as one of Kirk's officers walked forward under a flag of truce. Camp commander Lieutenant Bullock listened, I'm sure, in disbelief as we may imagine the Union soldier nearly shouted, "Captain Kirk, officer of the Third North Carolina Volunteer Infantry, demands the immediate, unconditional surrender of this camp." Bullock was in charge this day only because Major James R. McLean had taken personal leave the day before. Many of the two hundred Camp Vance recruits were still in bed.

From somewhere, a brave (or foolish) Confederate fired a shot into the woods. Others quickly joined him and the Union soldiers returned fire. As Bullock and his officers yelled "Cease fire!" the brief skirmish died down

In 1910 a granite monument dedicated to local Confederate soldiers was placed on the old courthouse square in Morganton. Several years later a surviving Confederate officer, Captain William Joseph Kincaid, donated the bronze statue that was dutifully placed atop the monument with its face to the north. *Author Collection.*

When Governor Holden was impeached in 1871, Lieutenant Governor Caldwell of Burke County assumed the office. Elected the following year, Caldwell encouraged the reopening of public schools that had been closed since 1863. Governor Caldwell died in 1874 while in office. *Internet graphic. N.C. Department of Public Instruction. North Carolina Governors Collection. 7 June 2007.*

with only a few men wounded. Bullock told the Yankee that the camp would surrender but he suggested Captain Kirk should respect private property and parole the doctors, staff and wounded. Fearing attack by the Home Guard at Morganton, Kirk ordered his men to move quickly and the Confederates were crowded onto the parade grounds. One company of Yankees went to Speagle's Turnout, destroyed the locomotive, three boxcars and the depot. Supplies were loaded onto confiscated mules and wagons as others set fires in the barracks, cabins and sheds.

Before the Union raiders approached the hospital, Doctors Merill, Whiting and Baker had been busy signing healthy men onto the sick list. Only by their "blarney and ingenious persuasion"[16] were they able to save the hospital, most of its supplies and protect some seventy men. It was at this point that Lieutenant Bullock and the Confederates learned of Captain Kirk's devious plan. Except for the doctors and men at the hospital, all others were to be taken under guard as prisoners of war to Knoxville.

In Morganton, Colonel Thomas Walton received word of the Camp Vance raid and called out the Home Guard to defend the town. A message was telegraphed to the Confederate prison at Salisbury, some fifty miles distant, and a contingent of prison guards was dispatched to intercept the Yankees. Kirk left Burke County by way of Piedmont Road, camping near Rocky Ford on the Catawba River the first night. The next morning, his band of marauders and prisoners continued into the hills toward Brown Mountain. It was here that a small company of regular Confederate troops from nearby Lenior, under the command of George Harper, caught up with the Union troops.

As the local story goes, Kirk placed his prisoners in the front line and a brief skirmish ensued in which the Confederate drummer boy Johney Bowles died. Kirk then moved to camp some twenty miles north of Morganton near Ripshin Mountain on Winding Stairs trail. On the next day, the Morganton Home Guard, Salisbury guards and others from around the area arrived to challenge the fleeing Yankees. Kirk, once again, had the advantage in defending this narrow path. During the brief fight, Kirk broke his arm and several men on both sides were killed and wounded. Colonel W.W. Avery of the home guard died from his wounds several days later in Morganton.

Following this encounter Kirk escaped, passed through Mitchell County where he burned Colonel Palmer's house and successfully returned to Knoxville with 132 prisoners, 32 African Americans and 48 horses and mules. Camp Vance was never rebuilt and within the next year this tragic war between the states ended with General Robert E. Lee's surrender in Virginia.

Stoneman's Raiders
Attack Morganton

The War Between the States was over. General Robert E. Lee had surrendered to General Ulysses S. Grant at Appomattox Courthouse in Virginia days earlier. But communications were slow and Union Major General George Stoneman did not receive this fantastic news. Just days earlier Stoneman's raiders, a force of more than four thousand cavalry, had invaded western North Carolina and destroyed the Confederate prisoner of war camp in Salisbury—something that U.S. Captain G.W. Kirk failed to do the year before after burning Camp Vance in Burke County.

Reminiscent of General Sherman's march through Georgia, Stoneman now moved his troops west from Salisbury destroying everything in its path. Military supplies were either confiscated or demolished. His troops were forced to live off the land and local farms were vandalized as animals, crops and foodstuffs were taken to feed his men and horses. The war in these last days had become desperate. Stoneman's soldiers wanted to end the fighting and return home. These raiders continued west along the Yadkin River and on April 15, six days after Appomattox, they reached Caldwell County.

In the small village of Lenior he stopped to rest and regroup. It was here that he heard about one more Confederate town in the area—Morganton lay only a few miles to the south across the Catawba River. Major General Alvin Gillem was ordered to take half the troops and march to Morganton. Stoneman turned the remaining army westward toward Tennessee where U.S. Major General John Schofield, commander of the North Carolina mountain campaigns, was headquartered.

As word spread about the Yankees in Lenior, the Burke Home Guard rallied to defend their communities. Perhaps fewer than two hundred boys and old men, for a second and last muster, assembled under the command of Colonel Thomas Walton with the assistance of two regular Confederate

Burke's Old Courthouse, constructed ca.1838 from local native stone to replace a wooden structure, was burned by "Yankee" raiders; therefore, all county records prior to 1865 were lost. Repaired with a stucco exterior and cupola, the building remained in use into the 1970s. It was restored in 1996 by the Historic Burke Foundation. *Author Collection.*

officers home on leave, Major General John P. McCown and Colonel Sam McDowell Tate. They dismantled the bridge near Rocky Ford and set up a defensive position with the only cannon in the area, a four-inch howitzer. Behind crude barricades they waited for Gillem's two thousand calvary.

On April 17, 1865, the Yankee column approached the river and gunfire began. The battle continued for some minutes, men on both sides falling dead or wounded. The Burke Home Guard held their positions until word came that the Yankees had outflanked them by crossing the shallow river upstream at Fleming's Ford. The Burke Home Guard that so bravely faced the charge now fled into surrounding forest and hills. Morganton lay ahead, unprotected, with women and children hiding in their homes.

Gillem's men spread out across town and countryside to pillage and burn. Farms some ten miles out were ransacked and stripped of animals and food stores. Camp followers with the Union troops, along with certain sympathizers from Burke's South Mountains, added insult to injury by vandalizing homes and stealing personal property. The only structure of substance in the county, the courthouse, was burned and with it most of the official county records up to that date. After completing their mission, Gillem's men moved west toward Marion and Pleasant Garden before returning to Tennessee.

As news of Appomattox became common knowledge, Burke County would once again be occupied by Union troops—this time to enforce the surrender of the Confederacy until 1868. Sam J. Ervin's study of the Civil War roster indicates that 1,285 Burke men were inducted into active military service during the war years, and among these, at least 500 were killed in battle or died from diseases. Many others served their time in Union prisons. The total population of Burke in 1860 was 9,237 with 2,596 listed as "colored."

Western N.C. Rail Road Changed Burke County

Over a century ago, Burke communities along our east–west railroad tracks could expect to see almost daily the arrival of steam locomotives huffing to a stop with freight and passengers. Railway passengers, however, have not gathered at a local train station for many years now, since Southern Railway stopped passenger service back in 1975. As a side note, state legislators in 2000 promised to return passenger trains to western North Carolina. In anticipation of this momentous event, major renovations to the Morganton depot were completed in 2004 that restored its 1916 appearance. In the meantime, curator Doug Walker, with the History Museum of Burke County, has furnished the building with artifacts that allow area citizens to see what the old days of steam locomotives were really like.

Before the railroad came to Burke County in the late nineteenth century, freight arrived by horse- or mule-drawn wagons and people came in coaches along with the U.S. mail. All of this changed in the 1850s following a long-term drought in western North Carolina, which caused extensive crop failures. Realizing that improved transportation was critical to the safety and future growth of these mountain counties, state legislators appropriated $12,000 to survey a rail route from Salisbury to the Tennessee line. Although the Western North Carolina Rail Road (WNCRR) was incorporated the next year, it would be several more years before construction actually began.

In the beginning, building the railroad was a joint effort among counties ($400,000), the state ($600,000) and several individual investors. Burke County had a stake in this endeavor as Robert Pearson of Morganton became the first WNCRR president and E. Jones Erwin and William Avery served on its board. By 1861 WNCRR tracks reached within a few miles of Morganton—but the War Between the States stopped construction on the

Western N.C. Rail Road Changed Burke County

A demand for lumber in North Carolina during the late 1800s was high and Burke County became a leader in cut timber and sawed lumber. After "the war" and the arrival of trains in Morganton, spur lines were built into surrounding hills to haul timber to sawmills. *Burke County Public Library, Picture Burke Collection. Al and Nelda Maxwell.*

The Morganton railroad depot, first constructed in 1886, was restored in 2004 to its 1916 appearance. Freight and passenger services were provided by the Western North Carolina Rail Road; chartered in 1852 it took almost three decades before its tracks reached Asheville. *Public museum jointly operated by the City of Morganton and the History Museum of Burke County.*

Lumberjacks and timber were big business in the second half of the nineteenth century. Wooden "shoots" were built to slide tree trunks down the mountain to a railroad spur. Small steam locomotive engines called "ponies" were used to haul cut trees to the main rail line. *Doug Walker Collection. Displayed at Morganton Rail Road Depot Museum.*

remaining route to Old Fort and Asheville. Soon after the war, with Burke Countians Samuel McDowell Tate as WNCRR president and J.W. Wilson as chief engineer, the train eventually arrived in Morganton; however, an official depot would not be constructed until two decades later.

In 1868 contracts were let for the difficult Blue Ridge Mountain section from Old Fort to the Swannanoa Tunnel at Asheville. The WNCRR would not arrive at Biltmore near Asheville until October 1880. Until then, railway passengers who continued their trip westward arrived in Morganton and rode a horse-drawn coach into these perilous mountains. Following certain financial difficulties in the early 1870s, the State of North Carolina purchased the WNCRR for $850,000. A few years later the railroad was leased by the Richmond and Danville Railroad of Virginia. Thereafter, the WNCRR ceased to exist (1894) when it became incorporated into the new and expanding Southern Railway system.

The heyday of passenger trains in Burke County came during the 1880s as our cool hills and enticing "mineral spring waters" attracted summer visitors from many distant places. Local entrepreneurs advertised the exotic and curative nature of Burke County's springs and created a small tourist boom at resort hotels named Piedmont Springs, Glen Alpine Springs and Connelly Springs. In his book *The History of a North Carolina County: Burke*, Edward Phifer Jr. reports that "invalids, the aged, and the infirm dominated the guest list."[17] He also hints that some of these spring waters may have been slightly enhanced with the addition of certain purchased minerals. Morganton, especially, was a bustling town of a few thousand souls who welcomed out-of-town guests at Walton House, Mountain Hotel and the Eagle Hotel. In addition, various boardinghouses catered to both local workers and itinerant travelers of all types.

In addition to tourists, the major Burke County industry during this period—timber—greatly benefited from the arrival of these locomotives. Chopped from our surrounding hills, then dragged by mules and horses to nearby sawmills, the trees were cut into lumber, loaded onto wagons and delivered to a nearby railroad track for transport. Eventually, several privately owned connector lines were built across Burke from the WNCRR to speed the transportation of both timber and lumber to meet an increasing demand in other parts of the state. By the beginning of the twentieth century, state officials were estimating that Burke County had depleted its forest and the industry was in decline. The appearance of automobiles and trucks in this new century, of course, foreshadowed an end to the considerable influence of the railroad in Burke County's history.

Community Names
Also Tell Local History

A recent conversation with Ann McCurry of Morganton about the correct name for Connelly Springs (or is it Connelly's Springs or Connellys Springs) in eastern Burke County, pricked my interest in other local community names I've heard about. After all, each of these villages and towns has a story to tell. A quick trip to the North Carolina Room at our local library, and the expert help of Gale Benfield, allowed me to leave with fourteen pages copied from a little red book entitled *North Carolina Post Offices and Postmasters*. This research becomes a bit tricky when you remember that a significant part of our county's history occurred in the earliest years of "Old Burke" between 1777 and 1842 when our boundaries extended from the piedmont into the Blue Ridge Mountains near Asheville. Eventually all or part of seventeen northwestern North Carolina counties would be taken from Old Burke, along with many of its original villages.

A quick look at the development of roads, stagecoach lines, railroads and the United States Postal Service provided an interesting perspective into the growth (and decline) of communities across Burke County during its two hundred plus years. Add to this the creation of other counties, politics and economics and you begin to understand why some of the post offices—and their communities—are no longer with us. Since its founding as a much larger county, Burke County has had more than one hundred post office locations, beginning with only one for many years (Morganton) and ending today with eight.

The first post office was established in Morgan Town in 1794 and remained the only post office until 1806 when Mackegsville between Morganton and Asheville (today McDowell County) acquired an office. Other present-day Burke County post offices include: Connelly Springs (first called Icard Station by the railroad) began as Happy Home in 1857. Glen Alpine was

Community Names Also Tell Local History

Connelly Springs Hotel was only one of several late nineteenth-century resort hotels in the county. Most touted the magical, medicinal properties of their "natural mineral spring waters" that attracted tourists from as far away as Charleston and Savannah. *Burke County Public Library, Picture Burke Collection.*

The Glen Alpine Springs Hotel opened in 1878 as the largest framed structure in the state. Built to accommodate one hundred guests, it offered luxury foods and services to those who traveled into the South Mountains by carriage from the railroad depot in Morganton. *Burke County Public Library, Picture Burke Collection. Greene Studio. Susan Fitz Rhodes.*

first known as Turkey Tail (1877), then Sigmonburgh and then Glen Alpine Station (not to be confused with an earlier "Glen Alpine" that became the now defunct Glen Alpine Springs). Rutherford College (1881), home to the county's first "college," grew out of the town of Excelsior. Icard came about in 1889 at Bowman's Crossing. Also in 1889, Drexel first appeared as Baker. Valdese opened a post office in 1893 after the Waldensians arrived from Italy. Hildebran at 62 Mile Siding came along in 1897.

By 1842 Old Burke was whittled down to a fraction of its original size as others received their portion. For example, Yancey County claimed Avery's Turnpike, Bakersville, Bear Creek, Grassy Creek and Youngs. Catawba County in the east inherited Chestnut while Caldwell County to the north absorbed Catawba View, Colletsville, Copenhagen, Dean's Mill, Globe, Harper's Store, John's River and Little River. McDowell County in the west received post offices at Locust Grove, Lovelady, Muddy Creek (which changed to Military Grove), Minersville, North Cove, Old Fort, Pleasant Garden, Turkey Cove and Wittenberg's.

In other years, as postal routes were consolidated, the smallest post offices in Burke County were discontinued. Some of these include Chesterfield (Hoodsville), Cold Spring, Enola, Henry River, Henessey, Jonas Ridge, Joy, Linville Falls, Lower Creek, Park Hill, Piedmont Springs, Rollins, Shell, Shoups Ford, Table Rock and Worry. Fonta Flora disappeared beneath Lake James. The following Burke County post offices were open for a period of fewer than five years: Burkemont, Canoe Creek, Clear Creek, Cothran, Frame, Gilmer, Gold, Janesville, Mace, Mana, Pearl, Penelope, Pitts, Valda and Waters.

During the War for Southern Independence, the Confederate States of America postal service only kept open those at Morganton, Brindletown, Bridgewater, Connelly Springs, Drowning Creek (became Pettigrew), Linville River and Perkinsville. Other circumstances place several communities among the lost and sometimes forgotten: Baird's Forge, Bedfordville, Brackett's Town, Camp Creek, Chamers, Dogwood, Eldridge, Flippersville, Whiteland and Warlick's Mills (which changed to Pearson then Warlick then Warlick Mills before being discontinued in 1905).

Moonshiners and Bootleggers

Ahistory of Burke would be incomplete without a few words on moonshiners and bootleggers. While this topic may conjure up colorful images of "revenuoors" chasing scruffy mountaineers through the woods, as usual there's much more to be told about this once popular pastime. First, we must distinguish between the manufacturer and the seller of illegal whiskey. The "moonshiner" (an old English term for "night worker") makes the whiskey, while the "bootlegger" (who once stuffed small bottles into his boot tops) sells it. The distinction between "legal" and "illegal" came in the late 1700s when a young U.S. Congress levied a tax on alcoholic spirits.

An immediate result of the excise tax on liquor was the Whiskey Rebellion of 1794 among Scotch-Irish farmers of western Pennsylvania. After a few federal agents were tarred and feathered, President Washington sent a military force of thirteen thousand troops to end the fracas—but not the problem. Following the War Between the States, the U.S. Treasury sent revenue men into the countryside to collect liquor taxes. To say the law was unpopular is an understatement; even North Carolina Governor Zeb Vance opposed the tax and described the revenuers as "red-legged grasshoppers."[18] An increase of the federal excise tax to $1.10 per legal gallon in 1894 created nothing less than a boom time for moonshiners.

Rondal Mull got me to thinking about this recently when he shared a bit of his family history. It seems that once upon a time in the late 1800s his great-grandfather was among a few state licensed distillers of whiskey in Burke County and this official document is on display at the History Museum of Burke County. However, it seems many years later one of his cousins found more pleasure (and profit) in dealing with the illegal sale of corn liquor. As Rondal tells the tale, "Ray" was the premier retailer of moonshine around

Home-brew beer, wine and liquors were necessities and a valued trade item among frontier settlers, but eighteenth-century tax laws prevented their sale by individuals. Some Burke citizens, however, continued the tradition as moonshiners or bootleggers—and eventually ran afoul of the sheriff. *Photograph displayed with liquor still at the History Museum of Burke County.*

Morganton—even during the Prohibition era. With his own private, labeled brand of "Burke's Best," Ray was a professional bootlegger.

"I suppose," states Rondal, "you could say that Ray was the first retailer in Burke County who had his own drive-in business."[19] On most Friday or Saturday nights you could drive a short distance out of town, circle to the back of Ray's house, stop at the bedroom window and call out your order. A hand would pop out the window with a pint or quart but no money changed hands. Several days later, Ray would spy his customers on the streets of Morganton and receive payment.

Ray was not a greedy man. In fact, he was something of a community philanthropist making regular donations to his Baptist church, the Boy Scouts and other good causes; however, the election of a new sheriff soon changed all this and Ray was dutifully arrested. With two of Burke County's finest lawyers in tow, Ray appeared before the North Carolina District Court judge in Shelby to plea for mercy—not justice. Attorneys John Mull and Frank Patton brought along many of Morganton's best citizens to testify on Ray's outstanding character. Finally, after three hours of hearing these pronouncements, the judge called a halt to the trial and asked Ray to stand.

In part, the judge stated that Ray was without a doubt one of Burke's outstanding citizens, but the evidence clearly indicated that he sold illegal liquor. "Mr. Mull, if I'm willing to release you, will you promise never to sell liquor again?" Ray quickly replied, "I will your honor!"[20] Ray returned to Morganton, quietly advertised a "going out of business" sale and started a chicken farm—never to be a bootlegger again.

You see, most frontier farmers during the early days of America made home-brew (beer), wine, brandy and/or whiskey for family medicine, barter, drinking and even cooking. Old-time fruitcakes were best when soaked in wine or brandy (as my Grandma Clark did). These customs and recipes were brought over with the earliest settlers and passed down from generation to generation. Therefore, farmers never quite understood an excise tax, and you must remember, unfair British taxes were a major cause of the American Revolution.

The early decades of the twentieth century became the heyday for moonshining in the Blue Ridge Mountains and the South Mountains of Burke County. The process for making corn liquor (white lightning, stump-water or rotgut) is fairly simple. Mix a pot of "mash" (cornmeal, sugar, water, yeast, malt) until it ferments and tastes right. Cook the mash to about 175 degrees until steam appears. Collect the vapors in a condensation tube and let the liquid drip into a container. The old mash, or "slop," may be reused up to eight times, with the addition of more ingredients. The clear, potent liquid produced can, according to certain people, clear your sinuses and kill any intestinal worms. In an attempt to personalize the flavor of their drink, a moonshiner's "secret ingredient" could include a little rubbing alcohol, formaldehyde or embalming fluid.

Although not common, bad batches of corn liquor were know to cause blindness (or death) among regular consumers, especially in later years when automobile radiators (with lead solder) were used as condensers. Another side effect could be "jake leg," a partial paralysis of one's legs—not to mention one's brain. Evidently none of these sad stories caused a decline in the demand for liquid spirits during Prohibition from 1920–1933. In fact, home-brew and bathtub gin became commonplace in both rural and urban areas. With passage of the Twenty-first Amendment to the U.S. Constitution, the prohibition against manufacturing alcoholic beverages ended and a new day dawned in America. If you can believe what's depicted in the Robert Mitchum movie *Thunder Road*, the long battle between revenuers and moonshiners now introduced faster cars (and NASCAR), the Mafia, bonded whiskey and state operated liquor stores. And, I suspect, a few diehard moonshiners that continue to practice their art and skill among the hills of Burke County.

Let's Name a High School for Robert Logan Patton[21]

W hile reading in the *News Herald* about a neighbor, Miss Margaret McGimsey, being honored by Mountain Grove United Methodist Church for her written historical account of the church and of the Women's Missionary Society, I heard from the deepest recesses of my mind the voice of Miss Margaret clearly say, "It's just awful that not one school in Burke County is named for Mr. Robert Logan Patton."

For those who know her, she is a walking encyclopedia on the families and events in the Table Rock area, and without encouragement speaks with great vigor and vividness about her experiences of some forty plus years as a career teacher in the Burke County schools. Some of those memories include Mr. "Logue" Patton who grew up in the shadow of Table Rock Mountain on the family farm located along Irish Creek in northern Burke County.

At a young age, Patton witnessed the death of his mother and the beginnings of civil war. He probably escaped serving the Confederacy only because it ended as he turned sixteen years old. The following year, he made a personal, momentous decision to leave his family with its drudgery of farm life to seek a college education. On that day, after rising before dawn to gather wood and start a fire in the kitchen stove, young Patton quietly left the house, passed the woodshed, picked up a bundle secretly stashed in the peach orchard the evening before and began his journey. In his own words written many years later in "My Struggles for an Education," Patton wrote, "On Tuesday morning, the 2nd day of October 1866, like Abraham, I started out I knew not where."[22]

Four days later he arrived in Jonesboro, Tennessee, but with no work available he walked on into Kentucky. Not until he reached Indianapolis, Indiana, weeks later did he find work, lodging and a suitable school. By

In the late 1800s students at Table Rock Academy sat with Headmaster Robert Logan Patton, seated front row left. Both a minister and educator, Patton served many rural churches and in 1903 became Morganton's first superintendent of public schools. R.L. Patton High School is his namesake. *H. Eugene Willard.* Images of America: Morganton and Burke County. *Charleston: Arcadia Press, 2001.*

April 1867 Logue was joined by his oldest brother and together they made plans to immigrate to Kansas. However, this idea changed when they reached Hillsboro, Illinois, where good wages and a fine academy kept them occupied for almost two years.

With the loan of $40 for train fare, Logue then followed his brother to Exeter, New Hampshire, to enter a private academy and prepare for enrollment into Amherst College in Massachusetts. His first years at Exeter developed into a pattern of late night studies, meager odd jobs, crackers and milk for meals and increasing debt. His life improved greatly while at Amherst with regular work, regular meals and an occasional scholarship. Logue finally realized his dream and his college diploma in June 1876 at the age of twenty-seven.

Now an "Amherst Man," Patton prepared to set out on another grand adventure—a return home to his native Burke County, and as the story continues, he arrived on Irish Creek with an armload of wood, greeted his father and said, "Here's the wood you sent me after eleven years ago." Thereafter, Patton served the citizens of his beloved foothills for almost fifty years as minister, teacher and educator. While his ministry is not a focus of this story, he nurtured a dozen different small country churches and gained some reputation as an apostle of alcohol prohibition and prophet of moral reform. In fact, his frequent public prayers for God's intervention were said by some to be responsible for the sudden death of Morganton's lone saloon-keeper, as well as the unexpected fire that consumed a local house of ill repute.

Patton is best remembered for his pedagogical career, first as founder of a school at Jonas Ridge and the Table Rock Academy in Burke and then the Globe Academy in Caldwell County. In later years he worked as a teacher in a variety of public and private schools and academies. In 1903 Patton was appointed as the first superintendent of the graded schools in Morganton. Thereafter, until 1912, he also operated a private school, Patton High School, in Morganton and at various times served as Burke County's superintendent of public instruction.

In a local address some years ago, another native son, Senator Sam J. Ervin Jr., remarked that "It would be impossible for anyone to magnify the work he did."[23] And as an example, Senator Ervin related how many of Patton's students became distinguished citizens as president of Peabody College in Nashville, president of Mars Hill College in western North Carolina, founders of Appalachian Normal School in Boone, a North Carolina superintendent of public instruction and missionaries to China, along with many school principals and school teachers. What a wonderful Burke County legacy to discover thousands of people across this region, state and nation touched by the life of one person—Robert Logan Patton.

Now we return to Miss McGimsey's original idea. Should we name a school for Robert Logan Patton? Should we name our schools for any individual? With certain restrictions, I believe that we should for two reasons: First, it is a way to perpetuate the memory of someone we admire for future generations to emulate; second, our youth today have far too few real-life, esteemed people to model their lives after. We could come up with a fine list of potential candidates as names for our new Burke schools, but we should begin with Robert Logan Patton, who promoted public education for all children and exhibited an extraordinary desire to learn.

The Waldenses of Italy—
and Burke

O ver a century ago Abram Joseph Ryan wrote: "A land without memories is a land without history." Among all of Burke County's citizens, Fred Cranford understood the importance of memories far better than most. As an educator, his passion for history brought Burke's past into the classroom and into the minds of our students. Following his untimely death in March 2007, Fred is now a part of our memories and of our heritage. It is Fred's words, both spoken and written, that linger with us, and hopefully remind us of the grand history that shaped this land—and its people. He was, after all, a storyteller.

While Fred worked in our public schools, he contributed much more to his job than asked, and thereby contributed to the larger community of Burke and North Carolina. A special interest for him became the exciting story about a small group of Italian immigrants who appeared here in the late 1800s, a people who left the crowded land of the European Alps for a new life in America—perhaps the last colonists to immigrate to North Carolina.

The Waldenses of Burke County was published in 1969 with federal grant funds as part of a Burke County Heritage Project. With illustrations by Jackie Deaton, Fred wanted everyone to read and remember the past suffering of the Waldenses in Europe and their achievements in our county. "It would be their efforts," he wrote, "that would change the face of Valdese from farm village to thriving textile town…[to] become known by 1938 as the 'Fastest Growing Town in North Carolina.'"[24]

So impressed was he with the valor of these Waldenses, Fred began to dream of bringing their story to life onstage. He became a leader in the revitalization of the Old Colony Players, which had existed between 1935 and 1942, and proposed the construction of an outdoor theater in

In the late 1800s a small group of Italian immigrants came to settle in Burke and build a new life in America. The Waldenses founded the village of Valdese, which developed into a thriving textile town within a few decades. Waldensian Museum, Heritage Winery and the Trail of Faith are located in Valdese. *H. Eugene Willard*. Images of America: Morganton and Burke County. *Charleston: Arcadia Press, 2001.*

Valdese. In 1968, as Valdese celebrated its seventy-fifth anniversary, the Old Colony Players performed the first stage production of *From this Day Forward*, a dramatic historical play written by Fred. In 2006 a short essay entitled "Waldenses of Valdese" appeared in the state magazine *Young Tarheel Historians*. Fred was very pleased that his story now had statewide readers among school students. During the 2007 season you were able to see *From this Day Forward* at the Fred B. Cranford Amphitheater in Valdese—the fourth oldest outdoor drama in the United States.

Back in the 1970s, Elizabeth Kincaid and Fred prepared several supplemental curriculum resources about Burke County history for classroom teachers. Later printed as a booklet entitled *Spotlight On Burke*, these materials brought many forgotten stories of the past to a new generation of students. During this same period, Fred wrote another play, *By the Time the Cock Crows*, that depicts a bit of interesting history surrounding the old courthouse built in Morganton around 1835, a building which served state judges and Burke County into the 1970s. As a new courthouse was finally occupied, some people began to debate the advantages of tearing down this dilapidated structure. Many people objected and the characters in Fred's play told the reasons why. In this story, after midnight, a group of "spirits past" gathered in the old courthouse to express their opinions about tearing down the structure. The audience heard the voices of Colonel Thomas G.

Walton and Sally Michael along with those of Davie Crockett and John Sevier express shame and dismay at such talk. Their ghostly opinion is best expressed by Issac Thomas Avery: "I think that we are all in agreement that when this courthouse is destroyed, a proud part of Burke County's heritage is destroyed with it."[25] With Daniel Boone's spirited threat to bring a Halloween night every night to anyone who tears the building down, the play ends.

Fred's love of history and Burke County reached far and wide. He actively participated in the development, fundraising and construction of the Trail of Faith in Valdese that depicts in concrete and wood the Italian homeland of the Waldenses. And in 2004, he joined a small band of local citizens in their efforts to create the History Museum of Burke County. This, he knew, would be the best way to save Burke's past for future generations. Burke County has lost an advocate and a friend—but Fred Cranford's voice will continue to remind us of our past.

Burke County
January 1, 1900

On January 1, 2000, Burke County experienced a spectacular, almost magical event as clocks ticked and time silently slipped by as the sun rose on a new day—a Happy New Year! Although this day included some misguided hoopla (it was not the beginning of a new century), I wondered what happened a hundred years ago when Burke County and the world experienced a similar occasion, marked another day off their calendars and found themselves in the year 1900. Obviously they had no concerns about a Y2K bug destroying their civilization.

The first newspaper to appear in Burke County that fateful year was the *Morganton Herald* on Thursday, January 4, published weekly at an annual subscription of one dollar, paid in advance. Its four pages contained abundant verbiage about the county, state, nation and world. There were no headlines or photographs announcing the New Year, but a front-page graphic of Old Man 1899 with the Young Child 1900 asked a question, "When does the 19th century end?" The Young Child responded, "Hold on, old fellow! I am coming and the nineteenth century will not be over until I have lived 365 days."

The front page also included articles about China's open doors ("opened" by the force of the world's major powers), General Buller and the Boer War in South Africa (many Americans supported the Dutch Boers against the British) and American troops chasing rebels in the Philippines (as they fought for national independence from the United States). "Telegraph Briefs" provided other tidbits from around the globe, including the one about Prussian (German) teachers being forbidden from hunting as a pastime because it was deemed to be immoral. "The Markets" column said nothing about the DOW but reported activities on the Charlotte Cotton Market. The announcement that North Carolina had released $100,000 to public schools indicated Burke would receive $907.68 in state funds that year.

Established in 1894, the North Carolina School for the Deaf continues to operate as a free day and residential facility for the education of children who are deaf or hard of hearing. Located on a beautiful and historic 160-acre campus in Morganton, their Rusmisell History Museum is open to the public. *Author Collection.*

The Western Insane Asylum of North Carolina opened in 1883 with one building and Dr. Patrick Livingston Murphy as superintendent. The hospital became a model in patient care with its "near normal home environment" through daily farm work, skills training and education. Eventually named for N.C. Governor J. Melville Broughton, a much smaller hospital continues to operate today. *Author Collection.*

A Methodist school at Excelsior after 1850 transformed itself into the Rutherford Academy and then Rutherford College under the stewardship of Reverend Robert Laban Abernathy. During the Great Depression, the college was acquired by Burke County for a high school. *Burke County Public Library, Picture Burke Collection. Greene Studio. Susan Fitz Rhodes.*

Its few advertisements encouraged Burke Countians to visit Leslie's Drug Store in search of Tolt's Liver Pills, "The Fly-Wheel of Life" and McElree's Wine of Cardul, "A Woman Only Knows." Price's Cash Store offered their one-cent specials for twenty-four envelopes, six Falcon pens or twenty marbles. Anyone remember Mexican Jumping Beans? In 1900 they were called "devil beans." The Brittan & Goodson Livery Stables was located in downtown Morganton while the Raw Fur House in Chicago waited for your shipment of hides. A special notice: "If you want further credit at Morganton Hardware, come and PAY WHAT YOU OWE."

In local news Miss Anna McGimpsey, recently suffering from typhoid fever, had improved satisfactorily. John Solomon, who died after "more than 90 years," was reported as the oldest citizen of Quaker Meadows. A "Resolution of Respect" signed by J.A. Lackey, O.M. Avery, T.R.C. McGimpsey, W.B. Avery and T.W. Drury from the Sunday school of Oak Hill M.E. Church, South, recognized the passing of brother William Marcus Winters. While bird hunting Christmas day, Thomas Smith accidentally "punctured" Will Warlick in the arm with a few pellets.

On the following day, *The Burke County News* arrived. This larger newspaper of eight pages contained mostly local and regional news. For example, Mr. Romulus Laxton and Miss Mary Tate were married Tuesday last by Reverend J.W. Jones, Miss Alice Collett provided a party to "quite a number of young people" Tuesday night and a son of Jason Roderick bought $15 of goods from Lazarus Brothers with a $20 Confederate bill as payment. He was arrested. That day, Lazarus was holding a winter sale that included men's suits for $3.75 to $8.75 and pants $0.95 to $1.98. Colored dress goods were offered for $0.39 a yard, silk for $0.49.

The Burke County News recognized the New Year with a reprint from a Raleigh *News & Observer* special edition that recounted the state's progress during the past year. Burke County was predicted to have a "very flattering" outlook for 1900. Morganton owned the local electric light plant and a new long-distance telephone company, which "served the people well." Located on the western line of the Southern Railway, Morganton passengers were only fourteen hours from Washington, seven hours from Raleigh and two hours from Asheville. The Gem Saloon, Eagle Hotel and a variety of boardinghouses catered to tourists arriving at the railroad depot.

With a county population of about twenty thousand in 1900 (now over ninety thousand), most employment was at the Alpine Cotton Mills, Lesh-Camp Tannery Company, Morganton Manufacturing Company and the Hogan Roller Mills. Timber and lumber remained major industries, although on a decline with the depletion of local forests during the past century. Over $30,000 had been recently paid for county gold mining properties. "The health of the place deserves more than a passing remark," stated the *News & Observer*, "situated on the sunny side of the Blue Ridge and 1,200 feet above the waves at Beaufort," its location led the legislature to select this area for a North Carolina Hospital for the Insane (later renamed Broughton Hospital) and the State School for Deaf Mutes of the White Race. (These developments prompted some thereafter to label Burke as the state's "western capital.")

This year of 1900 also witnessed the Waldenses, recent immigrants from the mountains of Italy, transforming the tiny village of Valdese into the "fastest growing town in North Carolina." With the exception of Morganton and its three thousand citizens, Burke was comprised of many small, thriving communities such as Nebo, Worry, Table Rock, Rollins, Pearson and Fonta Flora. In politics, Burke typically voted Democratic, and as expected, a majority voted that year for presidential candidate William Jennings Bryan and Cyrus Watson for governor, both of whom lost. Within a few short years cars replaced horses, state jobs replaced farming and steam engines powered new furniture factories and textile mills.

Legends, Myths and Folklore

In some ways Burke County is no different from most counties. Visit any small town long enough and someone will begin to tell you a few of their oldest stories of the "Believe It Or Not" variety. Burke has several that are strange or tragic or funny or spectacular—or a little bit of all these. Such are the things from which legends are made.

Along Highway 181 in the northern section of Burke County you find Brown Mountain. If you believe the tales told, there are mysterious lights to be seen on this mountain ridge since the beginning of history. Various reports indicate ghostly red, blue and/or yellow balls of light floating either above or alongside of Brown Mountain—or down in the valley. Depending upon the weather, you may witness one or many.

Brown Mountain has attracted worldwide attention with these mysterious reports. The U.S. Geological Survey conducted at least two studies with the conclusion that they were either locomotive headlights or marsh gases. Gerard de Brahm, a German engineer, claimed in 1771 that the lights were "nitrous vapors." There are even Native American stories of desperate wives bearing torches while searching for the bodies of dead warriors. And then there are the ghosts of those Yankees killed nearby on Winding Stairs or Ripshin Ridge. Take your pick.

There is a persistent legend that alludes to a war between the Cherokee and Catawba American Indians in the distant past that resulted in a joint agreement to declare this land we now call Burke, between the French Broad and Catawba rivers, as a common hunting ground with neither tribe allowed to build villages. Up in Caldwell County they have a similar story where, after a big battle, the two sides planted two "peace trees" that today are intertwined. This tale, if true, would conveniently explain why the earliest pioneers to the region (and Bishop Spangenberg) found no native villages here in the early eighteenth century.

While well known locally among bluegrass artists, Etta Baker did not record her first album until 1991. Thereafter, Baker was honored as a "National Treasure" by the Smithsonian Institution, along with awards from state and national folk music organizations. She died in 2006 at ninety-one years of age. *"Etta on Velvet" color portrait by Francis Hairfield. The Baker Family.*

Robert Roy Williams (1894–1931) ran away from home to become an actor. Following years of stage performances in New York City, Williams was called to Hollywood in 1927 where he became a star on the silver screen with Jean Harlowe in *Platinum Blond*. Williams died in 1931 from acute appendicitis. *Poster (1931). Columbia Pictures/Sony Corporation. Frank Capra, Director.*

During the War Between the States, Sarah "Sally" Michaels became famous for handcrafting a small clay smoking pipe valued by both Yankees and Confederates at a price of $0.25. Perhaps the county's first female entrepreneur, she lived in the South Mountains. *Photo displayed with soapstone pipe molds at the History Museum of Burke County.*

During America's War of Independence from the British Crown, Burke County men and women were deeply involved. The men are remembered for bravery in battle. The women, well, read on. British Loyalists often raided farms for food. On one occasion a Tory took Mrs. Thomas Lytle's new beaver hat and in turn received her caustic yell, (legend reports) "You'll bite the dust for that, you villain!" On another occasion at a farm near Silver Creek the British took a herd of sheep over the strong protest of a Mrs. Hemphill. The "bandits" escaped only to be followed by this wily woman. Once there, she convinced the officer in charge to return one sheep for her hungry family. As the story goes, she selected the old ram, which then led the entire herd back home. Also during the Revolution, Cherokee warriors raided settlements along Burke's frontier with encouragement and firearms from the British. In one attack, two Burke pioneer women, Mrs. Peter Brank and Miss Lydia Burchfield, were scalped, but recovered to live long and fruitful lives.

Francis "Frankie" Silver, the young mother of a baby girl, was hanged for murder July 12, 1833. She was convicted of hacking her husband Charlie with an ax and attempting to burn his remains in the cabin's fireplace. She never admitted to the crime (and the courts did not allow women to testify) but the prosecutor built his case around circumstantial evidence. Frankie's mother and brother were implicated but released. Appeals to save her were forwarded to the governor. After fourteen months in jail, her father and uncle designed her escape—but succeeded only briefly before she was returned to the "hanging tree." With almost two centuries of telling, there exists more twists and turns to the Frankie Silver story than a good-sized book can hold. Although repeatedly identified as the "only woman hanged in Burke County," in truth a female slave, Betsey, was hanged in 1813 as an accomplice in the murder of her master. Modern legalists suggest that Frankie was abused by Charlie and therefore committed justifiable homicide in self-defense.

Sarah "Sally" Michael was a pipe maker who lived in the South Mountains, perhaps acquiring this craft from her father. She became somewhat famous during the War Between the States for making a fine clay pipe with a wooden stem. It is said that both Yankees and Confederates far and wide valued her pipes at a price of $0.25. Made of local clay, Sally used soapstone molds to press the clay into shape and then air-dry. Thereafter the pipes were hickory fired, trimmed and finished. Her original molds are displayed today at the History Museum of Burke County.

Speaking of the South Mountains, which now are a state park, you can hear a variety of tall tales about this region of Burke County. During both the American Revolution and the War Between the States there are reports that certain families sided with the wrong side—later to be punished in one way or another. Then there's the bandit that holed up in a cave for years. Not even the sheriffs were foolish enough to attempt his capture. I suspect, however, that these hills are most famous (or infamous) for the illicit production of moonshine. Back in the olden days almost every family in Burke had a bottle of corn liquor around for medicinal purposes and a few continued well into the twentieth century selling their "surplus" supply to friends, neighbors and bootleggers. For these people, it was likely the only cash money they collected.

It seems that most freed slaves in Burke after "the war" began to acquire farmland and make an independent life for their families. John Moses Avery was from one of these slaves. Born in 1876, he attended the local school for Negroes and worked for a time as an orderly in Morganton's hospital. In 1898 John entered Kittrell College as a work-study student and graduated two years later with honors. For a few years he and his wife, Lula, operated the Waters Academy at Adako in western North Carolina, but with its failure John became an insurance salesman for the N.C. Mutual and Provident Association of Durham. By 1924 he was vice-president of the largest African American owned insurance company in the United States.

Natural disasters and accidents have, of course, occurred in Burke over the years. At the beginning of the twentieth century, Duke Power began to plan for the construction of dams on the upper Catawba River to contain a lake for hydroelectric power. As their workday approached in 1916, a proverbial storm of Bibical proportions arrived with days and days of rain that washed down the river, taking with it homes, bridges and livestock. It was luck that no one was killed. Again in 1940, another hurricane arrived from the Gulf of Mexico to flood the rivers and streams of Burke, though not as violently as its predecessor since Duke Power dams now helped to control the river. A repeat of this natural disaster has already happened twice so far in our new century with only minor damage.

As the next story is told, Fred Huffman, president of Drexel Furniture, on a hot summer morning in the 1930s noticed a company truck parked at a service station where its driver casually sipped a beer. Huffman stopped his car and fired Pat Poteat on the spot. As Huffman left the station for work in Marion, he realized that the loaded truck was still parked. Therefore, he turned around, arrived at the station and rehired Poteat to drive the truck to Marion—then fired him again. However, no one in Marion could drive the big truck, so Huffman rehired Poteat to drive it back to Drexel. Once there, Poteat was fired for the third time. Some time later Poteat applied for work at Drexel and was rehired and employed for many years. Pat Poteat eventually became mayor of the Town of Drexel.

Then there's the freight locomotive wreck in Drexel many years ago. Local opinion about its cause focused on a young boy that was playing near the tracks. As often told, the boy was taken to court but the judge became more concerned about the young fella's physical condition—a serious case of swollen tonsils that caused difficulty in speaking. Consequently, the judge sentenced him to visit a doctor and have his tonsils removed. Another historic event happened in 1893 as the town of Morganton burned to the ground. Without a fire department, people gathered to watch and save what could be saved from nearby stores. The Baptist Church, Hunt Hotel and seventeen other buildings went up in flames. It's interesting to add that photos do exist of a fire brigade pump company organized in earlier years, which somehow failed to arrive that night. A similar fate befell Burke's largest industry, the Kistler-Lesh Burke Tannery, early in the twentieth century. This large complex received thousands of hides from Chicago and Kansas City daily while Burke men hauled in oak tree bark to be used in the mill. Photographs of this disaster depict the factory consumed in flames—with Morganton's valiant firefighters on the scene.

Burke is Home to the "Master of the World"

When in Morganton, I occasionally stop by the Muses Bookstore on West Union Street to look for new publications written by local authors and books about Burke County. During one recent visit owner Shirley Sprinkle insisted that I must read *Master of the World* by Jules Verne, since it mentioned Morganton. Verne, however, was not from Burke County. He was a Frenchman. I'm not even certain he ever visited Burke County—but this book, published the year before his death in 1905, begins in North Carolina at "the little town of Morganton on the Catawba River."[26]

Jules Verne created the modern science fiction novel during the nineteenth century with *Journey to the Center of the Earth* (1864), *Twenty Thousand Leagues Under the Sea* (1870) and *Around the World in Eighty Days* (1873). His fantasies often dealt with scientific invention, ingenious machines and their potential effect on humanity—things that Orson Welles explored years later. Being something of a sci-fi aficionado, I've read Verne's other books and watched the movie versions umpteen times but never read *Master of the World*. What a pleasant surprise to discover that its hero, Federal Agent John Strock, arrives from Washington to investigate mysterious eruptions and rumblings on Great Eyrie, a "rocky and grim and inaccessible" mountain rising thousands of feet above Burke County near "the village of Pleasant Garden."[27]

We must forgive Jules Verne for his misplaced geography and colorful exaggerations, e.g. condors "wheeling and screaming above the peaks."[28] Even an "aeronaut" ascending in a balloon cannot reach Great Eyrie's towering summit. After all, Verne is writing for excitement—and for fun—and our Table Rock is simply not majestic enough for this writer.

As roaring nighttime fires periodically belch atop Great Eyrie, Agent Strock calls upon the mayor of Morganton to organize a team of climbers to lead him up the rocky cliffs. Could this be the birth of a volcano that will

Johnny Bristol left Burke County as a young man for the center of soul music at Motown in Detroit, Michigan. He gained some fame as a singer but also produced musical albums for others and wrote over three hundred songs—some for Stevie Wonder and Diana Ross. Bristol died unexpectedly in 2004 at age sixty-five. *Author Collection.*

Tall tales and yarns have been told since 1831 about the death of Charles Silver, his body found chopped into pieces and partially burned. "Charlie" Silver's grave at Kona in Mitchell County, therefore, has three markers for three separate burials. His wife, Francis, was convicted and hanged for the crime. *Author Collection.*

rain destruction upon western North Carolina? The climbers fail in their efforts and Strock returns to Washington to hear tales of other mysterious events around the country. A most extraordinary vehicle has been seen rushing along roadways in Pennsylvania, Tennessee, Missouri and several other states within days of each report. "Seen" is not the proper word, since no one actually saw the machine. Covered in a cloud of dust it simply roared pass them.

Burke is Home to the "Master of the World"

A leather tanning industry existed in Burke County for over one hundred years. The largest operation became the Kistler-Lesh Burke Tannery that opened ca.1900 and closed in 1948. Near disaster struck in 1925 when its bark yard burned. *H. Eugene Willard.* Images of America: Morganton and Burke County. *Charleston: Arcadia Press, 2001.*

Verne added to this mystery with news from Boston where a vessel appeared on the sea miles from the coast of Cape Cod. "The body moved with such lightning speed that the best telescopes could hardly follow it."[29] Could these strange events be related? At this point Strock receives a letter from Burke County. In part the brief note states "Know this: none enter the Great Eyrie; or if one enters, he never returns."[30] It was signed "M.o.W." As you might guess, there now appears a third machine on a lake in Kansas. Local newspapers report that the schooner *Markel*, while speeding under full sail, collided with an underwater object and nearly sank. Some people begin to speculate: After the mysterious automobile came the mysterious ocean ship. Now comes the mysterious submarine. (Isn't this story getting exciting? And the climax happens on Table Rock—a.k.a Great Eyrie.)

Washington now provides Agent Strock with all necessary resources to track down this mysterious inventor and his fantastic machines. Then, the second letter arrives addressed to the "Old and New World" from aboard the *Terror*. This message informed all governments that no fortune could purchase his machine and "Whatever injury anyone attempts against me, I will return a hundred fold."[31] This one was signed "The Master of the World."

Strock now implements a plan to trap the crazed genius. Federal gunboats almost catch the *Terror* on Lake Erie near Buffalo, New York. Thereafter his team of agents lies in wait for it to return; however, a second attempt at capture results in Strock being pulled aboard the *Terror*. To his amazement the contraption transforms itself into a flying machine to eventually land on the summit of Great Eyrie back in Burke County. Now trapped atop the great mountain, Strock identifies the Master of the World. He is Robur, once an honored member of the Weldon Institute of Aeronautics—and thought to have died years ago in a crash. Unable to escape, Agent Strock feels tragedy is near. Burke County—and the world—are in dire danger.

William George Randall
1860–1905

If fame is measured by the honors and recognition given to a native son by those outside of his home region, then Burke County has indeed been blessed with famous people that include Revolutionary War heroes, a spate of exceptional politicians, educators, preeminent jurists and attorneys, journalists, musicians, a historian and an actor or two. However, it seems Burke has produced, in all its history, only one prominent portrait artist.

William "Billy" George Randall grew up during the War Between the States and thereafter along Upper Creek in northern Burke County. As with most families, they eked out a meager living farming, fishing and hunting the rolling hills of the Blue Ridge, only occasionally traveling down the mountain to barter for supplies in the village of Morganton. His formal education in these early years was limited to attending "free school" for only short periods during the winter months. His parents, however, must have had a desire for their children to acquire more out of life, since in 1877 young Randall enrolled at Table Rock Academy located only a few miles from home.

Already a talented, self-taught artist, he enjoyed drawing lifelike portraits of friends and neighbors. One of these early sketches is of Reverend Robert "Logue" Patton, founder and teacher of Table Rock Academy. At one point, a group of Harvard geologists visiting Table Rock Academy was shown several of William's drawings and appeared to be quite impressed. Some time later, William received a package of paper and crayons from these visitors, the first art materials that he had ever owned. In the summer of 1880, William Randall boldly left the security of Burke County and his family to attend the state university at Chapel Hill. "Concluding that I was getting older faster than I was getting an education," he wrote, "I determined to go to the university and see what I could do."

William Randall (1860–1905), a graduate of Table Rock Academy, attended college and then traveled with his wife to Germany, England and France to study portrait painting. Randall returned to a studio in Washington, D.C., and later Raleigh before returning to western North Carolina. He died from tuberculosis. *Portrait by unknown French painter, Jim Beck family. On display at the Old Burke County Courthouse, Morganton.*

The only indication we have of Randall's continued interest in art is from a report about a classmate teaching him a technique for taking raised portraits from photographs. This knowledge allowed him to roam the piedmont region in his free time to earn cash as an "artist" to support his education costs. Following graduation, Randall taught school in McDowell County for a short time, and during his time there he married Annie

Goodloe. Declining an offer to teach at a Texas college, Randall and his new bride set out for New York City to accomplish his dream of becoming a professional artist. With continuing financial support from his wife, a teacher, they eventually made their way across the Atlantic Ocean to Germany, England and France. While in Paris, Randall studied under the well-known portrait artist Bouguereau and perfected his skills for bringing life to a canvas with his paints and talent. Upon their return to America, they lived for a while in Washington, D.C.

All too often the phrase "starving artist" is applied to those individuals who experience extraordinary hardships in search of a dream of becoming an artist. History is filled with many examples, and sadly this image also applies to William Randall. Poverty and the stress of living in foreign lands is only a part of his story. He and his wife Annie were the proud parents of three children, two of whom died in infancy and the third who died in early childhood. During all of his adult years, William Randall suffered an affliction from tuberculosis and his studio was often closed due to frail health and recurring bouts with this all too common dreaded disease.

Eventually returning to his home state of North Carolina, Randall opened a studio in Raleigh and began a productive career in the 1890s as a preeminent artist of prominent men in education, politics, business and law. One observer wrote that Randall's eye for beauty accentuated the charms of handsome women and "enabled him to paint pictures of children as few artists can." The portrait of North Carolina Governor Fowle resides in the governor's mansion while other works may be found in the North Carolina Museum of Art. More than one hundred paintings are thought to inhabit private homes from Washington, D.C., to Florida and of course several paintings are to be found at the University of North Carolina-Chapel Hill.

As the tuberculosis continued to drain energy and life from his weakened body, Randall and his wife moved to Arizona at the beginning of the twentieth century in search of curative treatments. Upon their return to North Carolina, they settled in Blowing Rock, he once again opened a studio and planned his funeral. Having recently celebrated his forty-fifth birthday, the end came on December 12, 1905. Burial took place at Glenwood Cemetery in Washington, D.C. Earlier, in a special 1896 edition of the Raleigh *News & Observer*, a host of accomplished state leaders were featured along with William George Randall. "In addition to his portrait work," the article stated, "Mr. Randall hopes to do genre work among his native mountains. What Millet has done for the peasantry of France, Mr. Randall may one day do for the North Carolina mountaineer." His portrait, by an unknown French painter, now hangs in the historic Old Burke County Courthouse.

The Lost Community of Fonta Flora

Once upon a time there was a small, idyllic village named Fonta Flora in western Burke County, nested in Linville River Valley within the shadow of Table Rock Mountain, Hawksbill and Shortoff Mountain. Houses, barns, fields, a store, ball field and horse racing track dotted these rolling hills. By the early twentieth century, Fonta Flora was a thriving farming community of perhaps one hundred souls that succumbed to rising demands for hydroelectric power. Lake James, named for cofounder of Southern Power Company (a.k.a. Duke Energy), was constructed between 1916 and 1923 with dams on the Linville and Catawba rivers and the acquisition of over thirty thousand acres for this project. Today, Fonta Flora lies beneath the blue, cool waters of Lake James.

No known photographs or paintings exist of the valley before impounded waters slowly covered Fonta Flora. We can only imagine the allure of this small community from its name—in Latin *fontis floris*—which suggests a valley with fountains of flowing mountain waters and beautiful flowers. Fonta Flora was primarily known before the War Between the States for its wagon trail to Lenior and Morganton. Sardis Church was a popular community meeting place, an interdenominational church for both blacks and whites. Hampton's "North Carolina Guide of 1877" mentions its post office but provides no count of its residents. By contrast, the nearest "incorporated town," Hickory, is reported with a population of 1,300 white and 175 black.

My interest in Fonta Flora was renewed recently when Nettie McIntosh shared a copy of "The History of African-Americans in Burke County." This booklet includes stories about the McGimpsey family that lived in the area and provides an interesting snapshot on an important period of Burke's past history. Riley McGimpsey and wife Christian Moore were born into

Rufus Morgan, a native of Virginia, photographed the western North Carolina mountains during the late 1800s for viewing as 3-D images in a stereoscope. A sometime resident of Burke, this scene of Linville River was included in Morgan's 1873 State Fair award-winning album. *Internet graphic. University of North Carolina-Chapel Hill Collection. 2 June 2007.*

slavery, worked on separate farms into their teens and married in 1871. Although Burke County's farms never attracted many slaves, its prewar timber, railroad and mining owners sometimes acquired hundreds of slaves. Freed from slavery after 1865, dozens of black families remained in the Linville area to prosper as sharecroppers, small business entrepreneurs and eventually property owners. They founded Shiloh A.M.E. Church in a log cabin and today continue a traditional annual weeklong Camp Meeting.

Riley and Christian raised eight children and enjoyed some twenty-five grandchildren. While they lived as most Burke Countians in those days as small-time "dirt farmers," Riley operated several other enterprises on the side. Records of Riley's transactions on file at the History Museum of Burke County include the regular sale of corn, wheat and molasses. By 1908 he was able to purchase an International Harvester binder and pay its $50 price in two years; it seems, by loaning/renting the equipment to others. Most likely he was involved in raising livestock and cutting timber as well. Their three oldest children (Cornelia, Joseph and Sarah) married and migrated to New York City; Joseph after graduating from A&T State University in Greensboro. A younger child, Margaret, attended High Point College, taught in Burke schools and then went to New York City to work as a child-care nurse.

The remaining children set their roots in Burke County and prospered. The youngest, Henry, worked as a lumberjack and on the Lake James dams that soon flooded his parents' home at Fonta Flora. After that, Henry operated a sawmill with his three sons. Through connections with nieces, nephews and cousins the heritage of Riley and Christian McGimpsey is found today across Burke County, North Carolina, and in several other states, including the McJimpsey's [*sic*] of Spartanburg, South Carolina.

As the waters of Linville, Paddy's Creek and the Catawba flooded little Fonta Flora, Nettie McIntosh writes "the people simply moved to the water's edge and settled."[32] Several prominent knolls, however, were not covered and one—a burial ground—is still tended today by those who remember. While Fonta Flora has been lost to view, its memory continues to live in the hearts and minds of its descendants. And its name has not been forgotten by others; for example, Lake James Cellars Winery produces a Fonta Flora blush and there's Fonta Flora Road in Nebo. Lake James Real Estate has a Fonta Flora development and the U.S. Department of Agriculture describes certain floodplains of the southern Appalachians as Fontaflora soils.

When Textile Was "the King"

During the colonial period, Carolina textiles were either imported from Britain or hand spun flax, wool and cotton yarn woven into cloth on home looms. Only after independence from the British Empire—and an end to the disruptions of Napoleon's wars—did Americans begin to produce textiles in quantities beyond basic family needs; however, it was the appearance of an industrial revolution in the New England states by 1800 that most benefited the rise of manufactured textiles. The Hargreaves's "spinning jenny" (1764), Arkwright carding machine (1769) and Cartwright's mechanical loom (1787), along with James Watt's steam engine and Eli Whitney's cotton gin, provided the wherewithal to operate a modern factory.

The first textile mill in North Carolina opened in 1813 in Lincoln County, but as yet did not signal the boom that would take this state into the twentieth century as a leader in textiles. As viewed by Brent Glass in *The Textile Industry in North Carolina: A History*, "it is worth remembering that North Carolina remained an agricultural state well into the first quarter of the twentieth century."[33] And it would be the piedmont, with its ample waterways for water-driven machinery and available poor dirt farmers (and occasionally slaves) as workers that garnered the most attention during the early nineteenth century. Steam power did not become a significant factor until around 1900 with the rise of railroads and cheap fuel from the state's timber industry.

While North Carolina chartered some fifteen small textile companies by the 1830s, it would be the 1850s before any textile mills appeared in the western counties of Catawba (Monbo Factory, Catawba Mill, Granite Shoals Factory) and Caldwell (Patterson Cotton Factory), most often financed by Northern capitalists, managed by Yankee engineers and using New England machines. Most mills produced only yarn for local consumption with any

Glen Alpine Knitting Mills Inc. (1920–1946) was only one of many fabric, hosiery, yarn and clothing textile mills to dot the local landscape during the twentieth century. Some national recognition was achieved by Shadowline, Skyland Textiles, Drexel Knitting, Valdese Weavers, Waldensian Hosiery and Alba Hosiery. *Burke County Public Library, Picture Burke Collection. Greene Studio. Elizabeth Michaels.*

surplus sold to Northern mills to be woven into fabrics. Before the War Between the States, North Carolina could list only thirty-eight cotton mills and seven woolen, while the town of Lowell in Massachusetts had thirty-one mills in production. It would take an agricultural collapse in North Carolina, brought on by severe drought, and a civil war to change this state's misconception that industrialization was something for other states to do. In 1890 less than 7 percent of North Carolina's workers were employed in all manufacturing but by 1915 the state had 318 textile mills with more than fifty thousand workers in this industry alone.

Burke County's colonial families followed a familiar history as almost every household had spinning wheels and looms to work primarily flax and wool. Very little cotton was grown or wool raised in Burke, and yet Dr. Phifer in *The History of a North Carolina County: Burke* states that in 1827 Jesse Hyatt operated a small cotton gin on Paddy's Creek and a wool carding mill was operated in 1870 by Charles Shuping and Frank Warlick. The first textile mill to open in Burke was the Dunavant Cotton Mill in 1888 near the Morganton railroad depot. Modern for its day, the plant was lighted with a ten-horsepower steam engine. Within a decade this financially troubled mill produced new owners and a new name, Alpine Cotton Mill.

A later attempt by John Meier of Charlotte to establish a hosiery mill among the Waldensians of Valdese failed on one hand but succeeded on the other. Meier, who departed Valdese for other ventures in North and South Carolina, was followed by Valdese brothers John and Francis Garrou. These two men learned the textile trade from Meier, came home in 1901 and founded Waldensian Hosiery Mills. Several years later with Antonine Grill and A.M. Kistler, the brothers organized the Valdese Manufacturing Co. to provide high quality hosiery yarn for the mills. John's son, John Louis, managed this operation after traveling to New England to study their factories. In that same year the Banner Knitting Mill, soon to be Martinat Hosiery Mills, opened in Valdese to remain in operation until 1964. The energetic Waldensians were also responsible for founding the Vaudois Hosiery Mill, Garrou Knitting Mills and others around Morganton. During the next several decades these mills, along with new textile companies, were liquidated or merged to create new corporations. Today Alba-Waldensian, Inc., with headquarters in Valdese, continues this grand textile heritage as the oldest manufacturing company to originate and operate in Burke County.

By the early twentieth century North Carolina became the leading manufacturer of textiles in the United States, built upon agriculture's success with King Cotton. This was the beginning of a monumental development in the history of our state, its people, its institutions, its culture and its ethos. Thereafter, the "mill village" became symbolic of the backbone in North Carolina's growth in manufacturing, and as some believed, "salvation for a downtrodden people"—especially for young girls and boys. The first mill village to appear in Burke was the Henry River Manufacturing Company founded by the Rudisills of Cherryville in 1905 as a water operated yarn factory. Steam power came in 1914 and electricity in 1926. The village built around this mill had a company store and houses for workers. The company ceased operations in the 1960s and today exists as an abandoned and forgotten ghost from the past. (See Diane Fields's splendid photographs at www.pbase.com.)

Other significant textile mills in Burke included the E.A. Smith Manufacturing Co. at Rhodhiss (eventually sold to Duke Power and later acquired by Burlington Industries) that made the first American flag placed on the moon. Not satisfied with only a sawmill, woodwork shop and furniture factory, Samuel Huffman and Dave Mull in 1913 organized Drexel Knitting Mill, which over the years merged with others to finally be acquired by Dan River Mills. The Icard Cordage Co., begun by Dave Mull and Bill Shuping in 1914, changed owners several times before its purchase by Samson Cordage Works of Boston in 1936. After World War II, the county witnessed the further expansion of textiles with many smaller mom and pop style "sock mills" opening—and closing—but together adding to the rise of textiles as the major manufacturing employer in Burke County.

Brent Glass wrote in 1992 that "the textile industry remains North Carolina's largest employer, and there are more textile workers in North Carolina than in any other state."[34] But time has a way of changing everything. During that decade of the 1990s problems began to multiply for the textile industry with "free trade" competition from foreign products and severe economic fluctuations in manufacturing and retail markets. These combined circumstances resulted in consolidation, bankruptcy, reorganization and liquidation of many textile companies across the nation as tens of thousands of jobs disappeared. For example, in 1995 there were 2,235 textile and apparel plants in North Carolina employing 252,704 people. Ten years later there had been a 37 percent decrease in the number of plants to 1,402 and a 61 percent decrease in employment to 97,525 workers. Today, Burke County and North Carolina continue to adjust to these devastating changes.

And When Furniture
Was "the Queen"

Before the War Between the States, only thirty-seven cabinet shops were listed in North Carolina. After the war, northern investors discovered our abundant supply of native walnut, cherry and oak needed for the shuttle blocks and spinning bobbins used in a rapidly growing New England textile industry. By 1900 there were hundreds of small wood shops in production across the state, along with forty-four furniture factories centered in High Point and adjacent counties. After the Sears, Roebuck & Company mail-order catalog appeared, North Carolina's furniture industry began to boom and the Southern Furniture Manufacturers' Association was organized "to promote harmony among manufacturers...[and] secure concessions in freight rates." With markets expanding worldwide, the Southern Furniture Exposition of 1921 displayed its best in a new ten-story building in High Point, an event that helped establish North Carolina as the "Furniture Capital of the World."

Burke County played a significant role in this budding business, specifically when two giants of the industry were founded here—Drexel Furniture Co. and Henredon Furniture Co. An earlier manufacturer was short-lived when the Morganton Furniture Co. (1885) was destroyed by fire; however, in 1910 a new company with the same name was reborn by local investors and W.H. Hall, an immigrant from New York.

Burke entrepreneurs Samuel Huffman and D.B. Mull in 1899 built a successful sawmill, then a sash and blind plant. As these businesses grew, houses were constructed for workers and the community took on the appearance of a new town in the heart of Burke County. Huffman asked Southern Railroad to suggest some names. From this list Huffman picked "Drexel," a family name in Philadelphia. By 1903 these two energetic men thought of a new venture and invited J.S. Abernethy, W.C. Ervin and

Drexel Furniture Company opened in 1903 and by mid-century became known as the "World's Largest Manufacturer of Quality Dining Room and Bedroom Furniture." Through various mergers, the company ceased to exist in Burke by the end of the twentieth century. *Large wall-sized aerial photograph ca.1950 at the History Museum of Burke County.*

A.M. Kistler to join them in creating the Drexel Furniture Company. From *Reflections: A History of Drexel Enterprises, Inc.* we learn that they began with two buildings and soon added a twenty-five-room hotel for workers. The first Drexel product line was a solid oak suite with bureau, washstand and bed for a wholesale price of $14.50.

Lady Luck did not last long when just three years later the Drexel scrap yard next to the plant caught fire and burned the entire operation. Both the owners and workers agreed to rebuild and within two weeks had 26,600 square feet of new factory space with new machinery. Over the next few years business was good—and getting better. By 1920, Drexel had sales of almost $800,000 and produced about four thousand bedroom suites per year. The company then acquired the Blue Ridge Furniture Company in Drexel and some time later the Teague Furniture Company in Marion. Also an industry leader in other ways, Drexel was among the first employers in North Carolina to provide group life insurance and an employee hospital plan.

In the midst of the Great Depression, the company experienced only one unprofitable year: 1932. This was also the period in which Drexel became the first in the industry to conduct a national advertising campaign and soon became America's best-known brand in bedroom and dining room furniture. During World War II, Drexel was a major supplier of desks, tent stakes and marine plywood for boats. The top-secret laboratory at Oak Ridge, Tennessee, received over four thousand bedroom suites. During the 1950s Drexel continued to grow with the purchase of Table Rock Furniture Co., Morganton Furniture Co. and Heritage Furniture of High Point. Drexel, itself, was purchased in 1968 by Champion International and over the next three decades acquired by various holding companies and corporations until 2001 when it became a subsidiary of Furniture Brands International, along with Broyhill and Thomasville. Today, Drexel Heritage Furniture Industries, Inc. has no manufacuturing plants in Burke County but exists with its corporate headquarters in High Point.

While a latecomer on the scene, Burke County's other leading furniture manufacturer, Henredon, has an interesting and exciting history. In 1945 Henry Wilson, Ralph Edwards, Don VanNoppen and Sterling Collett, star sales and operation managers at Drexel Furniture Company, decided to open a new factory. Henredon was from the beginning intended to be the very best furniture manufacturer in America, although its first product line consisted of only three chests. As a new player in the market, innovation became the key to their success. Retail customer services were enhanced with in-store demonstrations by Harry Jordon and Lefoy Rhodes. New products of the best materials and construction were proposed by talented designer Ken Volts. Marketing Director Lou Berry, among other achievements, signed a multidecade agreement with *Architectural Digest* for Henredon ads to appear on page two of every issue.

Corporate leadership constantly watched for advantages in production and in sales. An early partnership with Heritage Furniture of High Point proved profitable for both companies. Allen VanNoppen wrote in the *News Herald* years later:

> By the mid-1980s, Henredon employed more than a thousand employees who worked in wood and upholstery plants and offices in Morganton, Marion, Spruce Pine and High Point. Its cutting-edge collections, particularly its record-breaking Scene One contemporary group that utilized Italian finishing techniques little known outside of Europe, were in such demand that production was often sold-out before it began.

With famed architect Frank Lloyd Wright, Henredon was the first major furniture manufacturer to commission an exclusive licensed collection, the Taliesin Line. Thereafter, Henredon followed the path of so many other companies through acquisitions and mergers until it also became a subsidiary of Furniture Brands International Industries. As of September 21, 2007, local headlines in the *News Herald* announced the closing of all Henredon plants in Burke County with the loss of over five hundred jobs.

The last quarter of the twentieth century was an era when furniture was the queen industry in Burke County and across North Carolina with over two hundred manufacturers in the state and ninety thousand people employed. Serious problems, however, began to appear in the 1990s as "free trade" agreements opened American ports to furniture from around the world. Competition from Asian and Latin American producers with low-cost materials and labor (China: $0.69 per hour) caused American manufacturers to either close, merge or outsource work to countries within these regions. The result was a rapid decline in the number of North Carolina furniture jobs to fifty-eight thousand (35 percent loss) by 2005. Although North Carolina continues to rank third in the nation's furniture industry, Burke and neighboring counties continue to experience these negative trends among its people and economies.[35]

Seen a Good (Old) Magazine Lately?

I found an interesting old magazine recently. Well, I didn't find it—I bought it. In fact my son Alan sent an email suggesting that "eBay has something for you!" This internet auction house is one place I had never visited in cyberspace. Acquiring my 1941 copy of the *State* magazine (now know as *Our State*) proved to be rather fascinating. Click on eBay, read the notes, place your bid ($9.95 minimum!) and wait to see if you win. Three days later David Pittman of Raleigh emailed to say I got it (since I was the only one to bid anyway). Just mail the check.

I am now the proud owner of a sixty-three-year-old magazine, which will later be donated to the Burke County Library's North Carolina Room. This December issue, by the way, contains a feature story about Burke County, the reason I bid on it in the first place. Evidently, publisher Carl Goerch visited here and wrote the article. He begins by explaining that there is "Joy in Burke County, with Worry just five miles down the road," a reference to our two communities mostly settled by Hendersons. He also found local family names associated with Icard and Hildebran.

The *State* publisher was fascinated with Valdese being settled in 1893 by Waldensians from the Cottian Alps of northern Italy as well as the little community of Turkeytown—that now passes as Glen Alpine. Brindletown's gold rush days were also noted, along with our "Council Oak" of Revolutionary War fame at Quaker Meadows. He praised our industries in textiles and furniture (which in those days were BIG business).

This special report on Burke County attracted a number of local paid advertisements for the magazine from Waldensian Baking Company (since sold), Martinat Hosiery Mills(?), Henry River Mills (now a ghost town), Table Rock Furniture (defunct), Drexel Furniture (sold and closed), Valdese Manufacturing, Burke County Commissioners and the Morganton Chamber

Brown Mountain Beach, among others, has been a favorite local "watering hole" for almost a century. Seen here in 1936 are summertime enthusiasts enjoying cool mountain waters. This is near the area where Brown Mountain's famous "ghostly lights" are reported. *Burke County Public Library, Picture Burke Collection. Greene Studio. Susan Fitz Rhodes.*

of Commerce for "Mimosa City: Gateway to the Blue Ridge Mountains." Morganton was famous for its mimosa tree-lined thoroughfare, the annual Mimosa Festival and Mimosa queen. The mimosa trees, however, were killed by blight in the late 1940s.

Goerch also told a tale about taking dinner at the Caldwell Hotel in Morganton (H.P. Pitts, proprietor) where he spoke with Miss Beatrice Cobb, publisher of the *News-Herald* and well-respected newslady across North Carolina. Afterwards, they visited Judge Sam Ervin (father of Senator Sam J. Ervin Jr.) who provided many splendid stories about the North Carolina Superior Court sessions held in Burke County during the summer months between 1847 and 1861.

The next morning, Goerch traveled around the county with Will Davis and A.B. Stoney. Some of the photographs included several old Burke houses: Maplewood, where years earlier soon to be President Wilson spent his honeymoon; the James Erwin House, "Belview," built in 1826; and the McDowell House (mid-1800s) where later to be Governor Zebulon B. Vance married Miss Harriet Espy. They also visited the Connelly Springs Hotel, once famous among tourists for its "healing mineral springs."

"Burke County has one of the most interesting courthouses in the state… and one of the oldest," Goerch wrote. Built around 1835, it holds many interesting stories that include John Sevier's treason trial—and escape—as "Governor" of the new state of Franklin. This is also where young Frankie Silver was tried and convicted for the ax murder of her husband.

With a bit of tongue-in-cheek tone, Goerch ended his article with a pause "to give back to Burke County some of the things we borrowed from her a couple of months ago when we were writing-up McDowell County." It seems that his guide over there was so enthused about our beautiful foothills, the man implied that all before them belonged to McDowell County—including Table Rock, Linville Gorge, Wiseman's View, Brown Mountain and almost all of Lake James.

I really enjoyed reading this old magazine; however, a footnote to my pleasant stroll through Burke County's past includes a profound melancholy. This issue of the *State* is dated December 6, 1941. How many of you know what happened the following Sunday morning in the Pacific? It was "a day that will live in infamy"—if we choose to teach our young to remember.

Burke County Fair, One of the Best—Again!

O ur county fair celebrated its fiftieth anniversary in 2000, and once again people far and wide experienced one of the finest agricultural fairs to be found in North Carolina. As a tribute to the dedicated efforts of the Fair Board and its many volunteers I want to reprint an article I wrote for the second volume of *Burke County Heritage.*

Fairs and carnivals of various types have been held off and on in the county of Burke for over two hundred years. Edward W. Phifer Jr. records in his *History of a North Carolina County: Burke* that the first fair was held on the square in Morgan Town during November 1795. Farmers brought their best crops for bragging and selling. Children enjoyed candy treats. Elsewhere across the county, horse races were a favorite pastime at the end of harvest season. At this early date and into the next century, other community fairs appeared only rarely in North Carolina.

None was held during the Great Depression of the 1930s or the war years. Our present-day county fair, however, is now among the oldest since its reorganization in 1950 as an annual fair to "encourage and promote agricultural development and the mechanical arts." Those responsible for this rebirth included Ned Giles, Earl Searcy Sr., C. Miller Sigmon, James Beach, Harold Perry, Louis Garrou, G.T. Cornwell, H.G. Bobbitt, Frank Baker, Perk Reinhardt, J.H. Justice and Herbert Speas. Once chartered, its new home was at the Morganton High School ball fields and the National Guard Armory nearby.

Growth, however, later forced a move to Highway 70 near Drexel. This proved to be a disaster when rain on fair dates in two consecutive years produced little more than a monstrous mudhole and a $7,500 debt. On December 4, 1958, members of the Fair Board met with Salem Ruritan Club directors Ervin Ross, Lee Ross, Riley Fowler and Bill Digh to discuss

In 1927 Morganton Hosiery Mills opened in downtown Morganton specializing in ladies seamless and full-fashioned stockings. Pictured today, the original buildings recently underwent renovations to provide offices for the City of Morganton. Further renovations will soon provide apartments and small shops. *Author Collection.*

a plan for this club to assume responsibility of all fair operations. The proposal also included moving the fair to a new location and dividing any earnings three ways: one-third to retire the current debt, one-third saved for improvements and one-third for the Salem club.

Although Salem Ruritan approved the idea, they felt that this project was too big for just one club and soon thereafter held meetings with the other Ruritan clubs at Oak Hill, Chesterfield and George Hildebran. Each agreed to accept the challenge and a new Fair Board was created to include two members from each of the Ruritan clubs. Little did they know that many, many years would pass before any club realized income from their hard labor.

A new fairgrounds quickly took shape on leased Duke Power lands on Bost Road as Ruritan members constructed roads, walkways and new buildings. In addition to the annual fair, these twenty acres provided a much-needed location for several popular public events. Horse shows, music concerts, scout jamborees, the Soap Box Derby and famous demolition derby became regular attractions at the fairgrounds. In 1972, Johnny Clark became the first Ruritan member to be elected president of the Fair Board.

Disaster came again in 1985, not as rain but as Duke Power's Crescent Land & Timber, its new land management office, terminated the fair's lease and ordered everything removed within one year. Having few options for a new location, the Fair Board sought public support and asked Duke Power to sell the property. Although their first attempts failed to change the mind of Crescent Land & Timber, North Carolina Agriculture Secretary Jim Graham eventually joined our cause and used his considerable influence with Duke Power to acquire the present forty-two-acre tract for $131,000.

Previous savings, a bank loan and the considerable skills of local volunteer Attorney John McMurry resulted in a deed for the property. Afterwards, the future of our Burke County Fair improved considerably as the Fair Board paid the bank loan in three years, paved roads, constructed more buildings and finally provided a modest income to the Ruritan clubs for their many volunteer hours (and years) of work before, during and after each fair.

All of Burke County is indebted to the leadership of past presidents Clinton Foust, Ralph Dale, Jim Franklin, Worth Whisnant and Max Williams for creating and maintaining the fair for all these years, and to all those who volunteer their time and energy each year to provide us with an outstanding county fair and so many pleasant memories. When you see the current Burke Fair president—or any other officers—congratulate them and the Burke County Ruritan clubs for a great job. They deserve our thanks.

Senator Sam:
A Native Son Remembered

September marks the birth month of a Burke native who we should remember with a certain amount of respect and awe, since he stands among a select few recognized in the twentieth century as a vigorous defender of liberty and those individual American rights protected by the United States Constitution.

Samuel James Ervin Jr. was born in Morganton on September 27, 1896. The son of a prominent local lawyer and diminutive Southern belle, he would rise through the ranks of the legal profession from country lawyer to eventually serve as an associate justice of the North Carolina Supreme Court. Because of certain peculiar circumstances, he would earn not one but two law degrees along the way. After graduating from Chapel Hill and passing the North Carolina bar exam, he found himself continuing to pursue his wife-to-be by enrolling in the third-year class of Harvard Law School in Boston, Massachusetts. Two more years of romantic courting required him to next enroll in the second-year class and finally in the first-year class. Following this second graduation, he believed himself to be "the only person who ever went through Harvard Law School backward."[36]

As a veteran of World War I, "Sam" J. Ervin, Jr., was twice wounded, twice cited for gallantry and a recipient of the Purple Heart, Silver Star and Distinguished Service Cross. As a devoted Presbyterian, Ervin rose through the ranks of his religious faith to become an active elder of the session at First Presbyterian Church of Morganton. He would also rise through the ranks of politics from local Democratic Party chairman to serve as a state representative, U.S. congressman and eventually as U.S. senator. While in the U.S. Senate, he sponsored among other bills a Criminal Justice Act, Bail Reform Act and Bill of Rights for American Indians.

Local citizens recently erected a life-sized bronze sculpture of Senator Sam J. Ervin Jr. on the old Burke County Courthouse square. The Historic Burke Foundation and Morganton Public Arts Commission selected sculptor Alex Hallmark, who also crafted bronze busts for a recent World War II Memorial in Morganton. *Author Collection.*

Senator Ervin never missed an opportunity to defend the Constitution against perversions and stated on one occasion that "Ours is not a country in which government can become a tyranny against the will of the people."[37] It was during these years on the Senate floor that he gained a well-deserved reputation among his peers as a preeminent scholar of the U.S. Constitution. At a particularly critical point in American history during the mid-1950s, Senator Ervin was one of only a few Congressmen willing to denounce the slander and tyranny of the great Communist "Red Scare" instigated by Wisconsin Senator Joseph McCarthy.

Senator Sam, as he is fondly remembered in Burke County, also became popular for his wit and his inescapable quotations from the Bible, Shakespeare, major and minor poets and anyone else who would serve his particular argument at the moment. Read Ervin's own words in *Humor of a Country Lawyer* to understand the depth and breadth of what I mean. And, of course, it was his chairmanship in 1972 of the Senate Select Committee on Presidential Campaign Activities (at the ripe old age of seventy-six years) that ultimately brought him to the attention of the world. As it turned out, he was the right man at the right time to face the serious crimes and breaches of constitutional law emanating from the White House. As Senator Sam later stated: "The only security America has against anarchy on the one hand and tyranny on the other is to be found in reverential obedience to the Constitution by those entrusted with governmental power."[38]

Although under the constant glare of television cameras and of partisan scrutiny from both sides of the aisle, Senator Sam did his duty and delivered the committee's report to Congress only sixteen months after beginning the investigation. As a result, a host of Watergate burglars and White House conspirators went to jail. President Richard M. Nixon chose to resign on August 9, 1974, rather than face impeachment hearings by the Senate. Ervin retired from the U.S. Senate the next year with a remark that, "I wanted to return to the people who have known us best and loved us most, and watch the sun set in indescribable glory behind Table Rock and Hawks Bill mountains."[39] Of course the citizens of Burke County thought it only proper to welcome Sam and Margaret home and scheduled a festive event at the Drexel Community Center.

An interesting footnote to this "Welcome Home" party was to notice just how many young people were in attendance. In fact some wore "Uncle Sam" badges and T-shirts imprinted with the Senator's famous profile. Just as the original Uncle Sam with top hat and pointed finger called America's young men to war, Senator Ervin had achieved something like cult status among America's youth by reminding everyone that each generation must defend liberty and our democratic, constitutional system of government. His perspective was simple in that he believed that every American had a constitutional right to certain basic freedoms of citizenship without the interference of government. Our Congressional (and State) representatives would be wise to follow his sage counsel today.[40]

Spring!
It's Snipe Hunting Season

In the course of human events it appears that nations, states and other government entities at some point in their history decide to identify themselves with plants and animals. After all, the official symbol of the United States is a bald eagle (which narrowly won out over the American turkey). Likewise, North Carolina has an official bird (cardinal), flower (dogwood), mammal (grey squirrel), insect (honey bee), fish (channel bass) and even a dog (Plott hound). After more than two hundred years, I suspect it's about time for Burke County to select an official animal.

Just think on it. Burke's official logo would feature our certified animal on its letterhead and all county cars and trucks. Television broadcasts of commissioner meetings could open with our official animal proudly displayed. The county's Office of Travel & Tourism should promote this validated animal nationwide— even worldwide. But what animal should we select? Most common animals are already taken by states or other counties. Even the lowly possum belongs to Clay County, North Carolina, where they officially celebrate Possum Day by lowering one from a pole in a cage (alive) during their New Year's countdown, where in Burke County we often see this animal on our highways as roadkill.

So what "respectable" animal remains? Burke County deserves something better than a bug or fish! My recommendation comes from ancient Southern folklore—an animal associated with family and friends, one that connects us to Nature, a fun animal of storytellers—the sometimes maligned and forgotten "snipe." Locals report a few sightings of the Southern snipe near South Mountains, along the Catawba River and even on top of Table Rock. Sadly, I have yet to find one in Irish Creek Valley. Since none has ever been exhibited alive (they easily vanish shortly after capture), various anecdotal sketches depict a small mammal with a long, bushy tail, large eyes and pointed ears. I think its scientific name is *Raucous fundabus burkus*.

N.C. Governor Gardner presented this gavel to President Hoover in 1930 during ceremonies at the Kings Mountain battlegrounds. The gavel was crafted from a branch of the original "Council Oak" of Revolutionary War fame by students at the N.C. School for the Deaf. *Display at the History Museum of Burke County on loan from the President Herbert Hoover Museum in Iowa.*

Before you rush out to circulate petitions for our commissioners to adopt this logo, a word of caution. If you search the Internet for "snipes," you find Wesley Snipes the actor and film producer along with *Snipes*, the action-thriller movie set on the streets of Philadelphia. You may also come across "snipe," a bird kin to sandpipers, or www.snipehunter.com with its hunter's gear for shooting these flying birds. They ain't it. I speak of a far prouder tradition—an animal linked to generations of Southern youngsters as a rite of passage, a test of survival in the countryside on moonlit nights. The Southern snipe is a nocturnal, burrowing mammal that shuns humans to live in isolated backwoods or brush covered hills.

The only time you stand a chance to catch one comes on a full moon night, which some think is connected to snipe mating habits. Many techniques exist for search and capture but the most common requires a cloth sack. After a trained snipe hunter directs you to a suspected snipe hole, you lower your sack to the ground and mouth a series of clicking-sucking sounds to attract the animal. You stand alone, focused only on your task. No flashlights or torches are allowed, but if you get it right you feel the animal run gently into your sack. Since the Southern snipe is a very quick creature, you must be prepared to seal the sack immediately.

My first experience with hunting *Raucous fundabus* happened in Tennessee. I was maybe six years old when Uncle Glen, a mischievous teenager, took me out of Grandma Haun's backdoor into a nearby field. I still remember the crickets chirping and a crisp, cool moonlit night. As he later recounted the story, I stood patiently for some time making the snipe sounds when suddenly I ran like blue blazes back toward grandma's house. He almost yelled "stop" as I approached the barbwire fence, but I hit the ground on a dead run, rolled underneath and continued my sprint toward safety.

What I remember best about this adventure was when Uncle Glen returned with my sack in hand and said, "Larry, you ran off and left your snipe." Puzzled and amazed, I watched as he dumped a small, fluffy grey animal onto the floor. In my confused state of mind, I played with that snipe (kitten) for hours. This little misadventure with snipe hunting has, however, never diminished my belief in the noble snipe and I'm certain there are others in Burke County who hold a similar opinion. Perhaps a panel of knowledgeable citizens could explore the benefits of selecting the Southern snipe as our good luck mascot.

And perhaps, just perhaps, Burke County could designate an official day to celebrate the Southern snipe with poetry, song, dance and parade. Of course there must be a Snipe Calling Contest and the celebrations should end with an Official Sanctioned Snipe Hunt. There could even be a national competition—or international! Germans have a similar custom in Bavaria where they search for the *wolpertinger*.[41] Designated hunters would gather under a full moon at an appropriate location, be assigned a sector to search and, if lucky, return to the judges with their catch. Trophies, of course, must be awarded for the largest and smallest, the cutest and ugliest, etc. The possibilities are endless. Just think on it! Burke County could be unique in all the world.

Motorcyclists Love Ripshin Ridge

If you have traveled Highway 181 North during summer months, especially on weekends, you could not fail to notice an increase in the number of motorcycles—sometimes a dozen or more at one time. The attraction seems to be the mountain curves along this route, some 111 by my count in a one-way twenty-mile stretch.

Among motorcyclists (or "bikers" to some people), one of the must-rides in western North Carolina is Deal's Gap, down around Murphy and crossing over into Tennessee. This section of U.S. 129 in the Great Smoky Mountains is promoted as having 318 curves in only eleven miles. Well, I've ridden that road and must honestly say that I don't remember getting as many thrills as when I ride old Ripshin Ridge in Burke County.

Evidently, the word is finally getting around among flatland two-wheelers that our hills are more fun than those straight interstates down east—and much closer than Deal's Gap. Most motorcycle riders need only the slightest excuse to straddle their machines and head out onto the black asphalt that takes you anywhere and everywhere. Remember the motto of motorcyclists: "Ride to eat and eat to ride." Or on other occasions they may say: "It's not the destination, it's the ride." A flyer distributed by our local Gold Wing Road Riders Association describes this awesome Ripshin Ridge ride among our beautiful foothills of the Blue Ridge Mountains.

The measured route begins at Oak Hill, just north of Morganton, on Highway 181 and ends twenty miles up this curvy road at Jonas Ridge, a quaint community atop a mountain. This trail provides 111 real mountain curves (or 222 if you turn around and ride back) as you travel Winding Stair Knob and Ripshin Ridge where the elevation rises to over four thousand feet. Spectacular views of Pisgah National Forest abound (stopping to look is highly recommended), along with an opportunity to

In 1851 the state approved a wagon road from Morganton north into Watauga County. Although improved with tar and gravel early in the twentieth century, Highway 181 was not paved with asphalt until 1941 and celebrated by the governor and county officials atop the mountain at Jonas Ridge School. *Burke County Public Library, Picture Burke Collection. Greene Studio. Susan Fitz Rhodes.*

turn left or right, here and there, to explore the true natural beauty of Burke County's hill country.

The most obvious sights to watch for include Table Rock (3,909 feet high as seen from the skinny side), Hawks Bill, Long Arm Mountain (at 4,350 feet, the highest point in Burke County) and Grandfather Mountain (elevation 5,964 feet) off in the distance in Avery County. Also along the way are several out-of-the-way places that include the State Fish Hatchery, Wilson's Creek (a Wild & Scenic River national park), the ghost town of Mortimer, Linville Gorge, Linville Falls and Linville Caverns. Picnic spots and restaurants are to be found everywhere. Ride another three miles north and you arrive at an entrance to the Blue Ridge Parkway. Travel south on the parkway some fifty miles to Mt. Mitchell (6,684 feet and the highest point east of the Rockies) or travel north across the Linville Viaduct around Grandfather Mountain, the only raised mountain-hugging bridge road in the eastern United States.

Safety is always a primary goal among motorcycle riders and out-of-county visitors, especially the flatlanders, must anticipate what's ahead if they want to avoid trouble and have an enjoyable Ripshin Ridge ride. Some of these curves are easy while others are tricky. So on your first trip take it easy and enjoy—and remember that coming down the mountain is a different experience (read "more challenging") than going up. We certainly hope that riders on those racing cycles sometimes referred to as "crotch rockets" take to heart the advice of their peers and keep both tires glued to the road, avoid crossing "the zipper" in curves and wait to pass others only in the passing sections of the highway. You four-wheelers can take this trip in an automobile, but to really enjoy the beautiful mountain scenery of Burke County you need to have your face in the wind and the sun shining on your helmet.

Rejoice! It's Springtime in Irish Creek Valley

A pril is my favorite month among all others. This has happened, I suspect, because it is by far the most beautiful and peaceful time of the year along Irish Creek with no blustery winds or thunderstorms, no snow or freezing cold, no hot sun beating upon stagnant, humid air. Stated another way, as I view it, spring follows the gray, cold days of winter and comes before the dog days of summer. William Thackeray expressed the idea this way: "The rose upon my balcony the morning air perfuming, / was leafless all the winter time and pining for the spring."[42]

Burke's springtime sun is typically bright without being hot. Its brilliant rays sparkle in a Carolina blue sky and bounce among fresh, new flowers that beam with colorful psychic energies—vivid yellows of buttercups and forsythia, gleaming whites of dogwoods and pinks of budding fruit trees. I always wait with anticipation for the clever purple and astute gold of irises and lilies yet to come. The mornings are crispy cool and invigorating, preparing you for a new day.

As experienced by the poet Emily Dickinson:

> *A light exists in spring*
> *Not present on the year*
> *At any other period.*
> *When March is scarcely here*
>
> *A color stands abroad*
> *On solitary hills*
> *That science cannot overtake,*
> *But human nature feels.*[43]

For me, even mowing springtime grass is a pleasure, unlike August or September's brittle and dried stems. The tender green grass of spring flies and the air is filled with an unmistakable aroma of freshness and the promise of renewal. Here and there, clinging low to the ground you find last summer's weeds hiding among tiny fragrant flowers of lavender, yellow and white. In response to a child's question "What is the grass?" the poet Walt Whitman remarked:

> *I guess it is the handkerchief of the Lord,*
> *A scented gift and remembrancer, designedly dropt,*
> *Bearing the owner's name someway in the corners, that we*
> *may see and remark, and say, Whose?*[44]

The April air drifts in along Irish Creek Valley from Table Rock and other valleys faraway, carrying with it the unmistakable clean sweetness of springtime on its breath. It's at times such as these that we should satisfy our childhood urge for a walk into Irish Creek and rediscover the refreshing briskness of even cooler air bubbling from its sedate flowing waters. Perhaps, then, for a brief moment, we share something with William Shakespeare when he wrote, "But soft! Methinks I scent the morning air; brief let me be."[45]

April is also an occasion for some "work," such as planting your garden. The turned soil of spring has a delightful fragrance like no other. While Patricia and I no longer try to grow enough food to feed the family all year long, there is still something divine in eating fresh garden tomatoes or serving roasted sweet corn picked from your own plants. And don't forget the Southern custom of setting aside the first garden row for flowers. This splash of color serves as another reminder during later months of the miracle taking place in your soil. Charles Dudley Warner discovered that "To own a bit of ground, to scratch it with a hoe, to plant seeds and watch the renewal of life—this is the commonest delight of the [human race], the most satisfactory thing a [person] can do."[46]

Springtime in Irish Creek Valley also satisfies the requirements of artists for special landscapes, of philosophers for meditation and of the need for personal renewal. Such places permit us to commingle with Mother Earth, and hopefully escape the mundane and common. All we need to do is get outside and enjoy the beauties of April and spring. As John Milton reminds us: "In those vernal seasons of the year, when the air is calm and pleasant, it were an injury and sullenness against Nature not to go out and see her riches, and partake in her rejoicing with heaven and earth."[47]

You're from Burke County When…

We receive in the mail each month a copy of *Carolina Country*, a magazine produced especially for the 535,000 members of rural electric cooperatives across North Carolina and those Burke County residents served by Rutherford Electric. I find it to be a very informative and entertaining little magazine. One of the recent popular sections is entitled "You know you're from Carolina country if…" Readers by the score from across our state have sent in hundreds of responses to this open-ended statement. What's most interesting about these "folkisms" is that they tend to reflect the varied customs and slang sayings of each particular region across North Carolina—coast, piedmont and mountains—and most often deal with food, work, play, school, home and church.

Of course I like best those that speak about the Blue Ridge foothills and Appalachian Mountains—our part of Carolina country. So with many thanks to all those people who sent in their answers to *Carolina Country*, I wish to provide you with some thoughts that seem to speak to us in Burke County. Actually, the first responses to "You're from Burke County when…" comes from a Morgantonian, Lareen Beach, who observed: You know how to use a possum-hunting torch. You take deviled-egg sandwiches to school, not egg salad. You think an old coon dog is worth more than a registered fluffy lap dog.

To these, I add: You know who "Biscuit" is. But you're really from Burke when your favorite drink is SunDrop or Cherrywine and your favorite desert is a Moon Pie. You sometimes put peanuts into your RC Cola and know that "soda pop" is for Yankees. Southerners have been known to drink "dopes."

Tea is always served sweetened with sugar and any drink tastes better out of a Mason jar. Someone in your family makes grape wine or brandy "for

Postcards were once popular among local residents and tourists. This artistic Morganton card ca.1908 illustrates Broughton Hospital, Broadoaks Sanitarium, N.C. School for the Deaf and houses on West Union Street. *Burke County Public Library Picture, Burke Collection. Wayne Hitt.*

medicine" but no one admits to making moonshine. Sometimes you eat corn bread soaked in sweet milk for supper—but never at "dinner." A few brave souls actually use buttermilk. You also know the difference between red-eye, sawmill and Hoover gravy.

Your family never rides on the Blue Ridge Parkway in the fall to see the pretty leaves because all the flatland tourists clog the roads. You know that any slim chance of snow will close the schools. You also know that thunder in the winter means it will snow in seven days. On an election ballot Burke Countians would probably vote for Richard Petty or Ric Flair for governor. Everyone knows about UNC-Chapel Hill basketball, but no one admits to liking them. You still hide your Confederate money from the IRS.

In Burke county, we sell Krispy Kreme donuts for school or church fundraisers and know the difference between east and west BBQ—and the thick sauce is the only BBQ kind to use. Everyone eats lots of fresh 'mater sandwiches in the summer while a few folks like sliced cucumbers soaked in vinegar. Lard remains your favorite shortening. You know where to find creasy greens and poke salad in your backyard and always eat greens, black-eyed peas and hog jowl at New Years for luck.

Hunters believe that opening day for dove, deer or turkey season is a national holiday. You know what "cow tipping" means and when outside, how to avoid "cow pies." You can find a toad house or doodlebug. You can imitate the call of more than one animal and know what a polecat smells like. Your idea of a traffic jam is ten cars backed-up on the highway behind a farm tractor. Going to K-Mart or Food Lion is considered "going to town." You've had a "tar" blowout or caught something on "far." You know the exact distance to "over yonder" and "back thar" or you may tell people you live "a hoot and a holler away."

Burke Countians get most of their news—and make new friends—while standing in a checkout line at the store. You know exactly what someone wants when they say "give me a little sugar." You think "road rage" is drag racing on curvy mountain roads. You also believe that all Fourth of July parades must have tractors, horses, firetrucks, school bands and kids on bicycles. Now that's really Burke County. You got to love it!

Notes

Indian, Spanish, English, Irish, Scottish, Welsh, African, German
1. Augustus S. Merrimon, "Journal of the circuit beginning with the fall term of the Superior Court of Buncombe County, October 8, 1853," Appalachian Summit, http://appalachiansummit.tripod.com/chapt34.htm.

Native Americans of Western North Carolina
2. An extended version of this story first appeared in *The Heritage of Burke County*, Vol. II (Morganton, NC: Burke County Historical Society, 2001). Also see David G. Moore, *Catawba Valley Mississippian* (Tuscaloosa: University of Alabama Press, 2002) and Larry Clark, *Indians of Burke County and Western N.C.* (Morganton, NC: TimeSpan Press, 2002).

Way Back When Burke Was Part of Spanish Florida
3. On September 20, 1565, Menéndez captured the French colony of Fort Caroline, held its women and children for ransom and hanged the defenders. Several days later, near St. Augustine, Menéndez discovered over three hundred shipwrecked French soldiers and sailors. Most were killed by subterfuge and the sword. Albert Manucy, *Menéndez: Pedro Menéndez de Avilés, Captain General of the Ocean Sea* (Sarasota, FL: Pineapple Press, Inc., 1983), 41.

Captain Juan Pardo and the Spanish Empire
4. Arrell Morgan Gibson, *The American Indian: Prehistory to the Present* (Lexington, MA: D.C. Heath and Company, 1969), 111–112.
5. Charles Hudson, with Paul E. Hoffman, trans., *The Juan Pardo Expeditions: Exploration of the Carolinas and Tennessee, 1566–1568,* (Washington, DC: Smithsonian Institution Press, 1990), 57.

Lord John Carteret and the Granville Line
6. Archibald Ballantyne, *Lord Carteret: A Political Biography 1690–1763* (London: Essinger Publishing, 2004), 366.

250-Year-Old Diary Describes Old Burke
7. Adelaide L. Fries, ed., "Bishop August Gottlieb Spangenberg Original Diary and Notes," in *Records of the Moravians in North Carolina, 1752–1771*, Volume I (Raleigh, NC: Department of Archives and History, 1968), 28–64.
8. Ibid.

9. Ibid.
10. Ibid.

Quaker Meadows Presbyterian Church
11. For further information see Mark Andrew Huddle, *Lift High the Cross: A Bicentennial History of the First Presbyterian Church, Morganton, North Carolina 1787–1997* (Richmond, VA: Carter Printing Company, 1997).
12. Quoted in the *News Herald*, "Homecoming at Quaker Meadows Presbyterian," August 29, 2004.

Waightstill Avery—Patriot and Gentleman
13. Conversation with family historian Mary Lou Avery Furr at Swan Ponds. References found in the Avery Family of North Carolina Papers #33, Southern Historical Collection, Wilson Library, University of North Carolina at Chapel Hill.

André Michaux Slept Here
14. History of Grandfather Mountain, "About Grandfather Mountain: The Early Explorers," Grandfather Mountain, http://www.grandfather.com/about/history.php.

There's Gold in Them Th'r Hills
15. Col. Thomas George Walton, *Sketches of the Pioneers in Burke County History* (First published 1894 in the *Morganton Herald*; reprinted Easley, SC: Southern Historical Press, Inc., 1984), 37.

Confederate Training Camp Destroyed
16. Edward W. Phifer Jr., *The History of a North Carolina County: Burke 1777–1920, with a glimpse beyond* (Morganton, NC: E.W. Phifer, 1982 revised edition, ©1977), 327.

Western N.C. Rail Road Changed Burke County
17. Edward W. Phifer Jr., *The History of a North Carolina County: Burke 1777–1920, with a glimpse beyond* (Morganton, NC: E.W. Phifer, 1982 revised edition, ©1977), 285.

Moonshiners and Bootleggers
18. North Carolina Moonshine: A Survey of Moonshine Culture, 1900–1930, "Historical Overview," http://www.ibiblio.org/moonshine/drink/historical.html.
19. Rondal Mull passed this handwritten story to the author during February 2006, which was later published in a History Museum of Burke County newsletter.
20. Ibid.

Let's Name a High School for Robert Logan Patton
21. This column appeared in the *News Herald* in 1998. At least three additional articles in later years were devoted to promoting the tale of Logue Patton. In the fall of 2007 a new school opened in Burke County, the Robert Logan Patton High School.
22. Robert Logan Patton, "My Struggles for an Education" (later typed copy, n.d.), available in the North Carolina Room of Burke County Public Library.
23. Sam J. Ervin Jr., *Humor of a Country Lawyer* (Chapel Hill: University of North Carolina Press, 1983), 28.

The Waldenses of Italy—and Burke
24. Fred B. Cranford, *The Waldenses of Burke County* (Burke County, NC: Printed by Burke County Schools' Graphics and Industrial Communications students, 1969.), 26.
25. Fred Cranford, *By the Time the Cock Crows* (Morganton, NC: Burke County Schools, 1970).

Burke is Home to the "Master of the World"
26. Jules Verne, *Master of the World* (Mahwah, NJ: Watermill Press, 1985), 1.
27. Ibid., 2.
28. Ibid. 6.
29. Ibid., 33.
30. Ibid., 42.
31. Ibid., 57.

The Lost Community of Fonta Flora
32. Nettie McIntosh, "The History of African-Americans in Burke County" (Burke Co., NC: Committee to Preserve Black History in Burke County, 1996).

When Textile Was "the King"
33. Brent Glass, *The Textile Industry in North Carolina: a history* (Raleigh: Division of Archives and History, North Carolina Dept. of Cultural Resources, 1992), 30.
34. Ibid., 106.

And When Furniture Was "the Queen"
35. *Encyclopedia of North Carolina*, s.v. Furniture, (Chapel Hill, University of North Carolina Press, 2002).

Senator Sam: A Native Son Remembered
36. Heard by the author at one of Senator Sam's many public speeches and during the 2001 premier showing of *Senator Sam*, a one-act play at CoMMA starring Joe Inscoe.
37. Bill M. Wise, *The Widsom of Sam Ervin* (New York, NY: Ballantine Books, n.d.), 28.
38. Sam J. Ervin Jr., *The Whole Truth: The Watergate Conspiracy* (New York, NY: Random House), Prologue xi.
39. Read by the author in a *News Herald* report upon Senator Sam and Bess returning home, n.d.
40. Visit the Senator Ervin Room in the campus library of Western Piedmont Community College. It is here that you find a most impressive replica of the Senator's personal home office once located on Lenior Street in Morganton. All the furnishings—his desk, chair, hundreds of books, lamp, memorabilia, everything—are originals donated by his family.

Spring! It's Snipe Hunting Season
41. The Wolpertinger-*Crisensus Bavaricus*-(also called "Wolperdinger" or "Woiperdinger") is a mythical creature supposedly living in the alpine forests of Bavaria in Germany. It has body parts of various animals—generally wings, antlers and fangs, all attached to the body of a small mammal. *Wikipedia Online Encyclopedia*, s.v. "Wolpertinger," http://en.wikipedia. org/wiki/Wolpertinger (accessed September 20, 2007).

Rejoice! It's Springtime in Irish Creek Valley
42. William Thackeray, *Ballads* (Whitefish, MT: Kessinger Publishing, 2004), 66.
43. Emily Dickinson, *Collected Poems* (New York, NY: Barnes and Noble Publishing, 1993), 127.
44. Walt Whitman, *The Complete Works of Walt Whitman* (Hertfordshire: Wordsworth Editions, 1995), 31.
45. From Shakespeare's *Hamlet*, Act I, scene v.
46. Charles Dudley Warner, *My Summer in a Garden* (London: Samson Low, Marston, Low, & Searle, 1871), 21–22.
47. John Milton, *The Major Works* (London: Oxford University Press, 2003), 235.

Visit us at
www.historypress.net